W9-BSA-395

Books by Nathaniel Benchley

Side Street
Robert Benchley: A Biography
One to Grow On
Sail a Crooked Ship
The Off Islanders
Catch a Falling Spy
A Winter's Tale
The Visitors
A Firm Word or Two
The Monument
Welcome to Xanadu
The Wake of the Icarus
Lassiter's Folly
The Hunter's Moon
Humphrey Bogart

ILLINOIS CENTRAL COLLEGE
PN2287.B48B45
STACKS
Humphrey Bogart /

A12900 277980

A12900 277980

58047

PN
2287
.B48
B45

BENCHLEY
Humphrey Bogart

WITHDRAWN

Illinois Central College
Learning Resources Center

HUMPHREY
BOGART

KARSH, OTTAWA

NATHANIEL BENCHLEY, 1915-

HUMPHREY
BOGART, 1899-1957,

LITTLE, BROWN AND COMPANY — BOSTON – TORONTO

.C.C. LIBRARY   58047

PN
2287
.B48
B45

COPYRIGHT © 1975 BY NATHANIEL BENCHLEY
ALL RIGHTS RESERVED. NO PART OF THIS BOOK MAY BE REPRODUCED IN ANY FORM OR BY
ANY ELECTRONIC OR MECHANICAL MEANS INCLUDING INFORMATION STORAGE AND RETRIEVAL
SYSTEMS WITHOUT PERMISSION IN WRITING FROM THE PUBLISHER, EXCEPT BY A REVIEWER
WHO MAY QUOTE BRIEF PASSAGES IN A REVIEW.

FIRST EDITION

T 05/75

The author is grateful to the following companies for permission to reprint previously
copyrighted materials:

The I.H.T. Corporation, for an interview of Humphrey Bogart by Nathaniel Benchley, as
published in the December 8, 1940, issue of the *Herald Tribune*. Copyright, New York
Herald Tribune (I.H.T. Corporation).

The *New York Times*, for excerpts from the following movie reviews published therein:

"After All," December 4, 1931; "Chrysalis," November 16, 1932; "The Petrified Forest,"
January 8, 1935; all by Brooks Atkinson.

"The Big Sleep," August 24, 1946; "The Two Mrs. Carrolls," April 7, 1947; "The Treasure
of the Sierra Madre," January 21, 1948; "The African Queen," February 21, 1952; "The
Caine Mutiny," June 25, 1954; "The Desperate Hours," October 6, 1955; all by
Bosley Crowther.

Copyright 1931, 1932, 1935, 1946, 1947, 1948, 1952, 1954, © 1955 by The New York
Times Company.

LIBRARY OF CONGRESS CATALOGING IN PUBLICATION DATA

Benchley, Nathaniel, 1915–
    Humphrey Bogart.

    1. Bogart, Humphrey, 1899–1957.
PN2287.B48B45   791.43'028'0924 [B]   75-1384
ISBN 0-316-08886-2

Designed by Barbara Bell Pitnof

Published simultaneously in Canada by Little, Brown & Company (Canada) Limited

PRINTED IN THE UNITED STATES OF AMERICA

For Betty

who else?

T HE LITERAL-MINDED will complain that the quotes in this book cannot be accurate, and this is probably true. However, nothing between quote marks has been wholly invented; it has been put down to the best memory of people who actually heard or said what was said, and this is, in the opinion of the author, better than the indirect quotation that convinces nobody. The book is an attempt to bring life to what is rapidly becoming a legend, and to show the subject as he lived and breathed. Play it, Sam.

— N. B.

Hollywood/New York/London/Nantucket
1973–1974

HUMPHREY
BOGART

ONE NIGHT in July 1950, Humphrey Bogart and his wife Lauren Bacall were sitting with a friend in the old Romanoff's restaurant, in Beverly Hills. Perched on a barstool opposite their banquette was a man in the uniform of a Marine sergeant, and Bogart regarded him for a while in silence. The First Marine Division was just then embarking for Korea, and the general feeling was that as soon as they got there, the North Koreans would fold up and flee.

"That man's no Marine," Bogart said, at last.

"How do you know?" his friend asked.

"His hair's too long, and he's wearing white socks." Bogart looked for the waiter captain.

"Bogie, please," his wife said. After five years of marriage, Betty knew the signs of an approaching dustup, and she tried to head them off whenever she could.

"Pepe," Bogart said, as the captain approached. "Please ask the sergeant if he'll join us in a drink."

"Bogie," Betty said again, already knowing she'd lost.

The captain spoke briefly to the man at the bar, then returned. "He says no, thank you," he reported.

Bogart bared his teeth in a grin. "Now I *know* he's no Marine," he said.

"Bogie, please," said Betty.

Bogart looked around, trying to think of his next approach, but before he could do anything the man slid off the stool, bowed deeply, and flounced out as though he were walking on springs. Bogart laughed. "What did I tell you?" he said. "Let's go get him."

Betty managed to keep him seated until the man had a chance to get away, and slowly the idea lost steam. The evening ended with Bogart and his friend hotly debating whether or not there was an umlaut in the word *fünf*, the matter being settled only by a trip to the kitchen to find a German cook, who upheld Bogart's side of the argument. Bogart, who had briefly attended Andover, relished this triumph over an Exeter graduate who, in spite of having got A in German, was shaky on his umlauts.

Bogart's combativeness, which increased over the years, took many forms. Sometimes it was just testing, to see how a person would react; sometimes it was a definite needle, to puncture pomposity; sometimes it was a probe, to find out hidden fears or weaknesses; and sometimes it was simply for the fun of seeing the fur fly. His detractors pointed out that, no matter how loud or tough the talk, he never struck a blow and always avoided being hit himself, and in this they were correct because that was the point of the game. His friend Nunnally Johnson, the screenwriter and director, overheard him explaining it to Betty at Romanoff's one day at lunch, when Betty had observed that one of these days he was going to get his bloody head knocked off.

"You don't understand," Johnson remembers him saying. "It's an art. You do it sitting down or with glasses on, and bring it just to the point where he's

going to slug you, then you stop. It's the knowing where to stop that's
the main thing."

Johnson's theory, which is probably as good as any, is that Bogart liked to
think of himself as Scaramouch (a name that literally means "skirmish"), a
stock character in the *commedia dell'arte* who was the archetype of
deviltry, boastfulness, and cowardice. As to why he chose to do this a number
of theories have been advanced, most of them having to do with rebellion
against Hollywood. His detractors also maintained that he never picked on
anyone who could fight back, and this is simply untrue; he met more than his
match in John Steinbeck and Lucius Beebe, to name a wildly disparate
pair and only two of the several who bested him. On his first meeting with Sid
Luft, Judy Garland's husband and a man with a reputation as a handy type
with his fists, Bogart said, "They tell me you're a producer. What makes you
think you have the taste to be a producer?"

Luft's reply was instantaneous. "I have more fucking taste than any
cocksucker in this room," he said. Bogart fell, weeping with laughter,
into his arms.

To some people this game was infuriating — there are still those who go white
with rage at the mention of his name — and to some it was simply a minor
irritant, more boring than anything else. And then there are those who feel he
was doing the right thing, and that anyone he picked on richly deserved it.
And, on the other side of the coin, he could be funny and tender and gentle,
most often when it was least expected. He was a man with many sides, some of
them contradictory, and people's memories of him are naturally governed
by which of those sides they saw. As one of them put it: "How can a man, who
inspired as much love and loyalty as he did, have been such a sadistic
bastard?"

It's an interesting question.

IF EVER A MAN was gently born, it was Humphrey DeForest Bogart.

His mother, Maud Humphrey, was a portrait artist who specialized in children; her paintings graced the covers of *Delineator, Buttrick's* magazine, and the like; the "Maud Humphrey Baby" became as well known as the Arrow Collar Man, the Petty Girl, or the Schweppes Commander, and the children's books that she illustrated are now sacred items to collectors of such things. A tall, handsome woman with reddish hair and a strong jaw, she gave the impression of being stern, but her sternness was mitigated by the fact that she was terrified of butterflies. Penny weighing machines drove her into a rage, and butterflies drove her screaming for help; she was a complicated person but she was strong, and she was determined, and in later years it was she who supported the family.

His father, Dr. Belmont DeForest Bogart, was in many ways her opposite. Dark-haired and handsome, he was a man of great charm and professional ability, but with a knack of doing things that never turned out quite right. A horse-drawn ambulance had toppled onto him during his days as an intern, and thereafter his health was on the precarious side. (His legs and ribs were badly damaged.) But this didn't prevent him from pursuing a successful career as an internist, and the money he made was supplemented by a handsome inheritance, most of which he invested in timberland in Michigan. As a summer retreat he had a country place on Canandaigua Lake, in the

Maud Humphrey Bogart and her four-month-old son.

Humphrey DeForest Bogart at an early age, sketched by his mother.

Age two. Considering the size of the cuffs, his dungarees probably lasted him
until he was seven.

Finger Lakes of western New York State (both he and his bride were upstate
New Yorkers), and as his formal residence a brownstone house on 104th
Street, toward Riverside Drive in the city. Those were the days when a Riverside Drive doctor was the equivalent of the present-day Park Avenue
doctor, and a man who could boast that, plus a middle name like DeForest,
could well be said to have it made.

Into this genteel atmosphere Humphrey was born on Christmas Day, 1899.
He later would boast that he was "a last century man" — which in
many ways he was — but he had exactly one week in which to let the nine-
teenth century rub off on him. Photographs show a cherubic baby, with
dark hair and large, dark eyes, with an apparent willingness to smile at anything. Two years later a sister, Frances, was born, and two years after
that another sister, Kay, and that completed the Bogart ménage. (Although
Frances grew up tall and slim she was originally fat; "Fat" became her
brother's name for her, and that changed gradually to "Pat," which was her
name thereafter.)

For eight years Humphrey attended Trinity School, a large pile of gray stone
on 91st Street between Columbus and Amsterdam avenues. The boys wore
blue beanies with a gold TS; the pink-faced rector, Lawrence T. ("Bunny")
Cole, wore a flowing black cassock with a large gold cross that swung
loosely and bumped against his stately abdomen, and the daily chapel ser-
vices included incense and litany and everything in the book except
confession. If a student were fresh or otherwise out of order, the older boys
took him into the gym, where they threw a wrestling mat across the
parallel bars, put him inside, then beat the mat with iron dumbbells. After a
few years at Trinity School, a youth could laugh at Marine Corps basic
training. Humphrey, however, was taken to and from school by a nurse, which
cut down on his extracurricular activities.

11

Dr. Bogart's hope had been that his son would go to Yale, and to that end he was given a rounding-out year at the Phillips Academy, in Andover, Massachusetts. Andover and its rival sister school, the Phillips Exeter Academy, pride themselves on not having any rules until they are broken, and while this is not precisely true, they do make an attempt to let the student form a few judgments for himself. (Over the Academy Building door at Exeter is the legend HVC VENITE PVERI VT VIRI SITIS, exhorting all boys to come hither that they may be men — how they will change it now that girls are admitted remains to be seen.) On September 22, 1917, Humphrey was set down in this new world. The autumn foliage was ablaze, all around him were strange boys who seemed to have known each other for years, and while there is no record to prove it the chances are he was miserably homesick for the first few days. A picture of him at the time shows a handsome, scowling youth with a large upper lip and his hair parted in the middle, holding a pipe and assuming an air of uneasy repose. He is someone you would immediately choose for your athletic team, but might hesitate about asking to join the debating team.

During Thanksgiving vacation that year, he and his sister Pat attended a dance in New York, and there met Stuart Rose, a dashing young cavalryman on leave from the Army. He was five months older than Humphrey; he lived ten blocks north of the Bogarts on Riverside Drive, and he was so impressed by Pat that he corresponded with her on and off throughout the war, and later married her. He and Humphrey became close friends.

Humphrey made few friends at Andover; he was quiet and withdrawn, and gave the impression of being bored by everything. To the best of any of his contemporaries' memories he never cracked a book, and his consequent failing grades brought nothing more than a shrug. The one thing that interested him was the regular bull session on the third floor of Bishop Hall, where a youth named Floyd Furlow held forth in a witty and engaging style. Furlow's father was president of the Otis Elevator Company; his room was always well stocked with things to eat, and the conversation was wide-ranging and exciting. One of the group had worked on ships before coming to

At one of the bull sessions on the third floor of Bishop Hall, Andover. Humphrey is second from the left, his head on the bosom of an anonymous member of the Class of 1919. Floyd Furlow, the guru of these sessions, is near the apex of the pyramid in the rear, to the right of Jerome Bartlett, '20, his roommate. The only other identifiable student is Bob Brown, '18, on the far left.

About 1917, at
Andover. His liking
for dogs started early,
but the pipe was a
passing fad.

Andover, another hailed from South Africa, and Humphrey's greatest delight was simply to lie on the floor and listen to the talk. Arthur Sircom, who lived on a lower floor in Bishop Hall and also attended the sessions, thought of Humphrey as a dull, rather unfortunate fellow, who was blasé and naïve at the same time, and above all vulnerable; he had a "don't fence me in" attitude, and considered himself slightly above the law. In Sircom's words: "He did not fancy burying his searching eyes in *books*," and was, in sum, not cut out to be an Andover man.

The reasons for his eventual departure are clouded, and at this remove impossible to straighten out. Sircom remembers well his exit, and the conversation that went with it. It was a Thursday in May 1918, and Sircom was going from a class to Bishop Hall. He saw Humphrey coming down the path, carrying two suitcases and looking sullen, and Sircom asked if he was leaving for a weekend that early in the week.

"No," Humphrey replied. "I'm leaving this goddamned place, and for good. It's a waste of time here."

Sircom watched him go down the road to the station, his bags bumping against his legs, and he thought to himself, "You poor guy, you've ruined your life." For him, Andover was the greatest thing there was; he played the violin and was a leader in all the musical activities, and for a boy to split from such a place was like jumping off a cliff. Sircom later went on to be a theatrical and motion-picture director, and often ran into Humphrey around the New York theaters, but he never mentioned his thought on that day.

This, on the face of it, would make it appear that he simply quit, but in later years, referring to the academy, he said, "The bastards threw me out," and his widow recalls his saying he was caught coming in a window after hours. So the real reason is probably a combination of everything; any boy who was failing five subjects was on, to say the very least, thin ice, and a minor transgression could well have taken on major proportions. The odd thing is that, as time went by, he began to develop a warm feeling for the place he had ostensibly loathed, so much so that his widow enrolled their son Steve in the academy when he reached the appropriate age.*

The spring of 1918 was a restless one for many American youths. The war fever was burning brightly, the casualty lists were negligible, and the big cry was to kick the Kaiser back to Berlin. Some few, like Stuart Rose (who was with a machine-gun company at the front), knew what the war was really like, but for most of the country it was just the charge up San Juan Hill on a larger scale. The atmosphere when Humphrey arrived home from Andover was what might best be called strained, and in less than a week he went down to the receiving ship U.S.S. *Granite State* and enlisted in the Navy. Under the heading of Nautical Experience on his papers he put "Sail & Motor 2 years," and this reflected his summer sailing on Canandaigua Lake. The sailing, which he learned early, was a recreation that served him the rest of his life, and provided a weekend escape from the more cluttered tribal rites in Hollywood. Parenthetically, at the time of his enlistment the Canandaigua place had been sold; his father's Michigan logging venture had turned sour, and the financial squeeze was slowly beginning to tighten.

A month later he was sent to the Naval Reserve Training Station in Pelham Park, New York, where he received his basic training and from which he emerged with the rate of Coxswain, with orders to report to the U.S.S. *Leviathan*. (The *Leviathan*, originally the German liner *Vaterland*, had been interned in Hoboken at the outbreak of the war, and with American entry was seized by the Treasury Department and converted into a troopship. She was named *Leviathan* by President Wilson, and became irreverently known as *Levi Nathan*, or simply *Levi*. She could hold 14,500 men, and was by far the largest transport in the US forces.)

Humphrey actually reported aboard the *Leviathan* on November 27, eighteen

---

* As a footnote to his departure from Andover, the current legend, as relayed by an undergraduate, is that he was discovered by a member of the faculty to have a woman in his room; that he lifted the interfering instructor over his head, carried him to the nearest duck pond, and threw him in. The obvious inconsistencies in this story need not be pointed out; the narrator added, somewhat wistfully, that Andover has a scarcity of famous Old Boys, and tends to magnify the exploits of those they can rightly claim.

Humphrey in the early autumn of 1918, when he emerged from the Pelham Park Reserve Training Station with the rate of Coxswain. Shortly after this he acquired the famous scar that gave him his lisp.

days after the original orders, and by this time his rate had slid back to Seaman 2/Cl. It seems reasonable to assume that it was during this period the incident occurred that literally left him scarred for life. In later years, publicity releases and program notes would say that his lip was cut by a piece of shrapnel while he was manning the wheel of the *Leviathan*, or that it was a wood splinter torn loose by shrapnel; these ignored the fact that the war had been over for sixteen days when he reported aboard ship, and that even the most delayed-action shrapnel would have had to be traveling in a vertical line, either up or down, to nick the right corner of his upper lip and leave the famous scar. What actually happened was that, while waiting out his period of shore duty, he was assigned to take a prisoner (Navy, not German) from somewhere in the south up to Portsmouth Naval Prison, in New Hampshire. The man was handcuffed, though not to him, and when they changed trains in Boston he asked Humphrey for a cigarette. Humphrey cheerfully complied, and while he was producing a match the man raised his manacled hands and smashed him across the mouth, and fled. Humphrey, his lip torn almost off, whipped out his .45 and dropped the man as he ran, and by the time the prisoner was secured in Portsmouth and Humphrey had been treated by a Navy doctor, he had the makings of a lifelong scar. The doctor was apparently a frustrated sailmaker, and three subsequent plastic surgery jobs failed to undo the damage he had done when the wound was fresh. It was concealable onstage, but the probing eye of the camera never failed to show it up, and it lent an air of menace to an other-wise pleasant face and was probably responsible for his slight lisp. The lip was always big, and the lisp might have occurred without the scar, but Stuart Rose says flatly that Humphrey did not lisp when he first met him. Looking at him in movie close-ups, when he is enunciating clearly, you can see the lip moving out, almost like a proboscis, to envelop a word, and then returning to lie wetly against the teeth while a new word is being formed.

He served aboard the *Leviathan* until February 15, 1919, when he was trans-ferred to another transport, the U.S.S. *Santa Olivia*. Any ship was a come-down after the *Leviathan*, and with the end of the war a good deal of the glamour of being in the Armed Forces evaporated, and morale and moti-vation were not what they had been when the fighting was at its fiercest.

But even at the most gung ho of times there are always those who make it a game to see who can be last aboard the ship before it sails, and it would appear that Humphrey was one of these. (The probable all-time winner was an officer in World War II who, having run at flank speed the length of Duval Street in Key West, cleared a widening eight feet of open water to land sprawled across the rail of his submarine chaser.) Humphrey was, at that point, drawing down a fat $39.50 a month, and it's conceivable he decided to blow it all in one night on the town; whatever the reason, when the *Santa Olivia* sailed for Europe on April 14, 1919, it sailed without him. He turned himself in to the Navy authorities in Hoboken, the port of departure, and was transferred to the receiving ship in New York. This prompt action on his part expunged the "Deserter" that had automatically been stamped on his records when he missed the ship, and the offense was commuted to A.W.O.L. He got three days' solitary on bread and water, and the matter was closed.

On June 18, 1919, he was honorably released from active duty as a Seaman 2/Cl. During his period of duty his fitness reports, based on a scale of 1.0 to 4.0, with 2.5 considered passing, were 3.0 or above in proficiency, and 4.0 in Sobriety and Obedience.

And then, like thousands of other veterans, he started looking for a job. One problem was that the idea of business repelled him. His father had influential friends, and through them he tried two or three jobs — he took a stab at the National Biscuit Company, and there is a report he had something to do inspecting tugboats — but the whole thing seemed pointless to him, and he never lasted at one place very long. He was simply a very nice young man with a pleasant singing voice (one of his favorite songs was an English music-hall ballad: "Every Saturday afternoon I love to go to the Wax Works Show, and see my dear old mother; I likes to think of her as she was the night she strangled Pa") and none of this made him eminently employable. He preferred to hack around with his friends, and it was through his friends that he eventually — and literally — bungled his way into a career.

20

Among the Bogarts' neighbors were William A. Brady, the theatrical producer; his actress wife, Grace George; and their children, Bill Jr. and Alice. Humphrey and young Bill had been friends for a long while, and they often killed time clowning around the Playhouse, Brady's theater on 48th Street. Stuart Rose joined their group and, being an ardent horseman and graduate of the Cavalry School, he did what he could to interest them in horseback riding. Young Bill was a reasonably good rider, but Humphrey had never been on a horse, so Stuart took him in hand and taught him the rudiments, and later said that of all the people he'd taught it was Humphrey who learned the fastest. Beautifully coordinated, he was a natural athlete ("and a damn good wing shot, too," Rose adds), and he conquered his original nervousness so quickly that he never had any trouble. He and John Cromwell, the director, and a youth named Durham who was inevitably known as "Bull" used to ride in Central Park on Sundays and, parodying the hints in theater programs on "What the Man Will Wear," togged themselves out in burlesques of spiffy riding gear.

Another member of the group was Kenneth MacKenna, a quiet, shy young man who Grace George thought had strong possibilities as an actor. He shared quarters with his brother, the stage designer Jo Mielziner, in a remodeled brownstone on Waverly Place, a few doors east of Sixth Avenue, with Jo having his studio in the front and Kenneth having the rear part of the floor. This was, apparently, an ideal place for parties, in which Jo recalls Humphrey as taking an "active" part. (This is one of those tantalizing adjectives that will probably forever resist clarification. Heywood Broun, fired from the *World* for "disloyalty," wrote that "Disloyalty, unexplained, could mean anything from robbing the till to sitting on Ralph Pulitzer's hat"; by the same token, saying that a man took an "active" part in any backroom festivities could mean anything from statutory rape to singing Gilbert and Sullivan's "Three Little Maids from School Are We." Humphrey had a nice voice, and would on occasion entertain his friends with impromptu singing, but at the same time he was never one to back away from a more adrenal type of frolic. Prohibition was in force, and any red-blooded American youth did whatever he could to defy the forces of Puritanism. And, as a double parenthesis, all his friends from the early days called him "Humphrey," "Hump," or "Humph"; the "Bogie" nickname didn't creep in until the later Hollywood years.)

According to the memories of their contemporaries, it always seemed to be Humphrey who inherited Kenneth's girls after Kenneth had lost interest and/or headway, and this pattern wasn't changed until many years later, when Kenneth married the second Mrs. Bogart following her divorce from Humphrey. Taken all in all, the activities of the group were intramural to say the very least. At this, or perhaps a slightly earlier (or later) time, an actor-to-be named James Cagney appears to have been somewhere on the scene, but he feigns amnesia about the entire period, and the final word must await publication of his memoirs.

Alice Brady, an accomplished actress in her own right, was slightly older than Humphrey, and she took a maternal interest in him. She asked her father to give him a job, and Brady, more to please his daughter than out of any conviction that Humphrey was worth anything, made him an office boy. There followed a variety of positions, including a disastrous stab at directing a picture, and finally, in 1920, Brady gave him fifty dollars a week to be company manager of a play called *The "Ruined" Lady*, which was going on tour.

A company manager is responsible for the arrival of the baggage, props, scenery, and actors, as well as the housing and general welfare of the company and, in short, everything except the play itself and the publicity, and

22

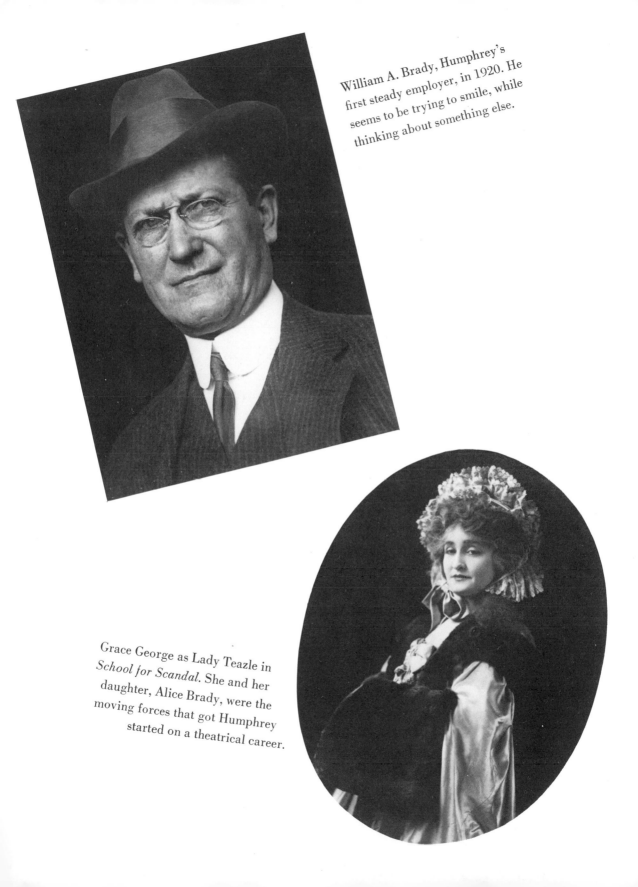

William A. Brady, Humphrey's first steady employer, in 1920. He seems to be trying to smile, while thinking about something else.

Grace George as Lady Teazle in *School for Scandal*. She and her daughter, Alice Brady, were the moving forces that got Humphrey started on a theatrical career.

Alice Brady, Humphrey's determined champion in the theater. On the back of
this picture she wrote, apparently to her press agent: "There is a highlight across
the bust that makes me look large — see if you can fix it — but you can use it
anyway — only if possible try to fix." By present-day standards, it's hard
to see what she was worried about.

Humphrey earned every dime of his fifty dollars. It seemed to him that actors were grossly overpaid for doing very little actual work — certainly memorizing someone else's words and then speaking them in turn couldn't be considered work — and he used to tease Neil Hamilton, one of the cast, about the easy life they led. Hamilton's reply was to arrange it so that Humphrey took his — Hamilton's — part on the last night of the run, and the result was traumatic. Humphrey had never been in front of an audience, and was unprepared for the almost tangible electric current generated by a house full of people; he was also unprepared for the apparent sincerity of the other actors in delivering their lines. He was literally terrified when another actor spun on him in a scene that called for a burst of rage, and he was moist and shaking when the final curtain spared him — and the audience — any further torture.

But Alice Brady had some notion that he could act, once he'd grasped the essentials. He was an eminently likable young man, ingratiating and well mannered, and he had the kind of good looks required for juvenile leads; all he needed was experience. She gave him a one-line bit as a Japanese butler in a play she and her husband, James Crane, were trying out at the Fulton Theater in Brooklyn, and it was a night that Stuart Rose remembers well. Rose had been in a Memorial Day parade with the National Guard, and he hurried home to change into civilian clothes, then went to the Bogarts' to pick up Pat and Dr. Bogart, and then the three of them went over to Brooklyn. The house lights went down, the play began, and after what seemed like a long wait Humphrey appeared, wearing a white jacket and carrying a tray of cocktails. He spoke his line (which is the only thing Rose can't remember), and Dr. Bogart gripped Rose's knee and whispered, "The boy's good, isn't he?"

"Yes, sir," Rose replied, wishing he'd never come. The boy was terrible.

Then Alice got him a part in *Drifting*, a melodrama in which she was starring, and he was listed on the program simply as H. D. Bogart. He played a character named Ernie Crockett, and beyond that nothing is known of his performance. The critics left him alone, which was probably just as well, but

Alice Brady in
Drifting, the play
that Alan Dale of the
New York American
called "strangely
protruberant."

of the play Burns Mantle said that it was something of a mishmash of "flashy melodrama," and Alan Dale called it "strangely protruberant." (Think that one over, and try to imagine what it means. Could a director tell an actor not to be so strangely protruberant? Could a playwright go to a producer and say, "I've written a play that's strangely protruberant and I think you'll be excited by it"? It's a shortcut to madness.)

Then, in the fall of 1922, Humphrey was assigned the second lead in a play Alice's father produced called *Swifty*, written by John Peter Toohey and W. C. Percival and starring Hale Hamilton. Humphrey's riding friend, John Cromwell, was the director. Cromwell had some inkling of what lay ahead when Humphrey came up with his first question: "Which way do I face — toward the audience, or toward the other actors?" He was, as Wolcott Gibbs once wrote about another player, totally innocent of the art of acting, but Cromwell's problems didn't end there.

The story, such as it was, involved an ex-prizefighter and a girl who had been deflowered in an Adirondack cabin by "a young sprig of the aristrocracy," and rehearsals weren't very far along before it became obvious they were in deep trouble. Ring Lardner was called in to see what he could do to avert disaster, but even he was unable to surmount the obstacles posed by the script as well as the acting. Humphrey, playing Tom Proctor, the aristocratic seducer, was batting into a wind that would have caused many an experienced actor to cringe, and his naïveté did nothing to make his part any more believable. The play opened on October 16 at the Playhouse, and the reviews next day were predictable. Oddly enough, Burns Mantle of the *News* rather liked it, but Heywood Broun, writing for the *World*, called it "cheap and implausible," and Alan Dale of the *American* said that "William Holden and Humphrey Bogart gave some rather trenchant exhibitions of bad acting." (This was not, incidentally, the William Holden who later appeared with Humphrey in two motion pictures. That William Holden was four years old when *Swifty* opened.)

But it remained for Alexander Woollcott, the critic of the *Herald*, to write the only review that Humphrey ever carried with him. Of the play, he wrote

Humphrey and Rose Hobart in
I Loved You Wednesday.

Edwin Nicander, Alice Brady, and Kenneth MacKenna in *Oh, Mama!*

Helen Haye, Margaret Perry, and Humphrey in *After All.*

that it was "a consistently incredible piece, a little more gauche and artless than the average of similar endeavors which slip past the tryouts in the suburbs," and of Humphrey's performance his opinion was that "the young man who embodies the aforesaid sprig is what is usually and mercifully described as inadequate."

Swifty folded in short order but Humphrey had, incredibly, decided to become an actor. No matter what the anguish, it was better than being a company manager, and Brady had told him that it was the actors and not the company managers who got rich. (This is not strictly true; the company manager of a big hit collects enough so-called "ice" to put his and all his relatives' children through medical school.) As for critics, Humphrey was later quoted as saying, "I always thought they were fair except for one, who wrote that 'So-and-so was bad in the part, but not as bad as Humphrey Bogart would have been if he had played it.'" That, he felt, was gratuitous.

Swifty started him off on a long string of juvenile roles, some good, some bad, and some simply window dressing. Richard Watts, Jr., recently retired critic for the *Post,* swears that he heard Humphrey, wearing a blue blazer and carrying a tennis racket, come onstage and speak the immortal line, "Tennis, anyone?" as the playwright's device for getting unwanted characters off the stage, but he cannot now remember the name of the play. Others tend to doubt that the words were ever spoken; they maintain they were symptomatic of the kinds of part rather than any one part itself, and Humphrey gave a different version every time the subject came up. Once he said his line was, "It's forty-love outside — anyone care to watch?" and another time he said he'd spoken every bad line except, "Give me the ball, coach, and I'll get you a touchdown."

It was a year after *Swifty* that he got his next part, that of a reporter in a comedy called *Meet the Wife.* It starred Mary Boland, who as early as 1923 was a well-established comedienne, and also in the cast was a young dancer-turned-actor named Clifton Webb. Both Webb and Miss Boland received rave notices, and the *World* gave Humphrey his first boost by saying that "Humphrey Bogart is a handsome and nicely mannered reporter, which is

Stuart Rose, later to become Humphrey's brother-in-law, as a first lieutenant at the Cavalry School in Fort Riley, Kansas, in 1922.

refreshing." It was in Eleanor Griffith's dressing room in *Meet the Wife* that he met Mary Philips, a young lady who in the course of time became his second wife. At that point she had only two plays to her credit, having been in the chorus of *Apple Blossoms* and had a speaking part in *The Old Soak*, but she went on to earn a solid reputation as an actress. She was also, and still is, a gay and charming person. She says of their meeting that "he must have taken a liking to me," but as things worked out it was five years before they were married. She remembers him as being something of a Puritan, impeccably polite and careful about his language.

The stage manager of *Meet the Wife* would have modified that description. At one matinee Humphrey unaccountably forgot that he had an entrance in Act III, and at the end of Act II he took off his makeup and went home, leaving an embarrassing gap for Miss Boland and the others to fill. When he showed up for the evening performance the stage manager asked him where the hell he'd been, and Humphrey, with no ready answer on his tongue, hit the man in the jaw. Miss Boland didn't speak to him for the run of the play.

In 1924 he and a group of his friends, all professionals of one sort or another, got together and put on a play called *Nerves*. It was produced by Bill Brady, Jr., written by John Farrar and Stephen Vincent Benét, and the set was designed by Jo Mielziner. The cast, aside from Humphrey, included Mary Philips, Kenneth MacKenna, and Paul Kelly. It was in two acts, the first being at a Yale house party during which several couples became engaged, and the second in the officers' mess of a flying squadron in France, during which the ins and outs of cowardice and heroism were explored. It opened on a rainy night in September, the night after the opening of *What Price Glory?*, and the comparison was invidious. Heywood Broun tried to be as nice as he could, but concluded that "according to my emotional standards *Nerves* is a bad play." He felt that it got better acting than it deserved, and said, "It seems to me that Humphrey Bogart gives the most effective performance. He seemed decidedly more real than any of the other Yale aviators." Kenneth MacKenna, on the other hand, "suffers from trying too desperately to make a feeble play take on the breath of life." Alexander Woollcott, writing of Humphrey's performance, said somewhat cryptically that "the authors could hardly have expected any-

The leading players in *Cradle Snatchers*. Left to right: Raymond Hackett, Margaret Dale, Humphrey Bogart, Mary Boland, Edna May Oliver, and Raymond Guion, the last of whom, after some thought, changed his name to Gene Raymond.

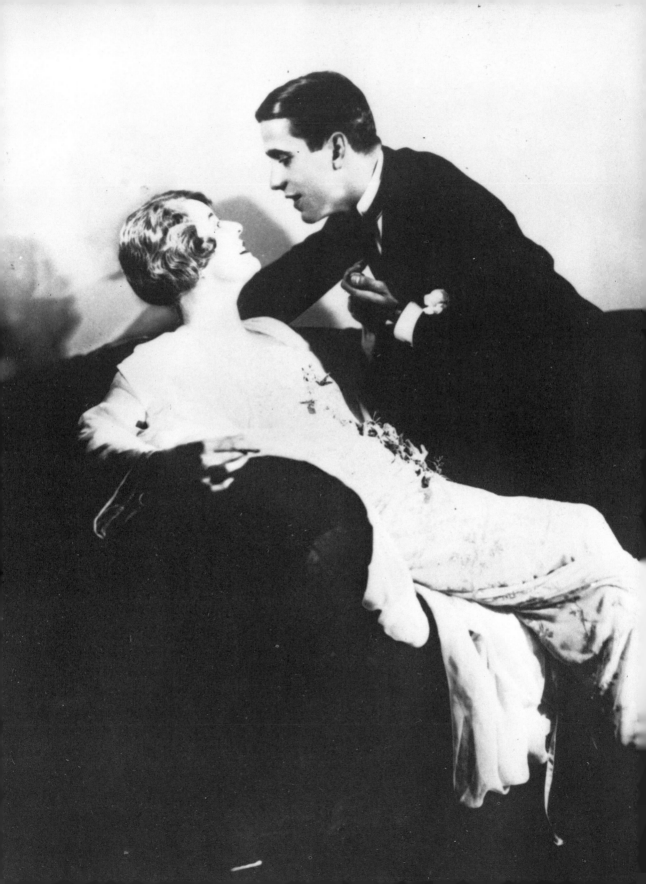

Humphrey and Mary Boland in *Cradle Snatchers*. The dialogue for this scene has unfortunately been lost.

Helen Menken, Humphrey's first wife, in *The Captive*.

thing better," which, in the context of the rest of his review, was not necessarily flattering. *Nerves* perished in short order.

During this period Humphrey was slowly learning his trade, and the results began to be apparent in the reviews. In January of 1925 he opened in a comedy called *Hell's Bells*, which the *Times* called "painfully synthetic," and the *Post* "foolish but harmless," but Alan Dale (he of the strange protruberance) gave it a rave, and said that one particular scene was "gorgeously acted by Violet Dunn and Humphrey Bogart."

Then, in the fall of the same year, a play called *Cradle Snatchers* was being cast, with Mary Boland as the star. Her status was such that she had the final word as to who the other players should be. They tried man after man for a certain role and none of them was satisfactory, and finally she said, "Oh, all right, then, get Bogart. I know it's what you have in mind." They did, and his first words to her after the two-year banishment were, "Hello, Mary." The incident was never referred to. The *Times* sniffed at the play but said the audience loved it, and listed Humphrey in the "further pleasing performances" category. This time it was the *World* that did the raving. The story, briefly, concerned three society matrons who decided to kick up their heels, and to this end they found a hideaway and equipped themselves with three gigolos. Their husbands eventually stumbled into the hideaway under the impression it was a high-class bordello (which in a manner of speaking it was), and all hell broke loose. The *World* chortled that it was a "raucous and bawdy farce," and went on to say that "the company is good throughout, but the honors go clearly to that enormously comical actress, Edna May Oliver, to Mary Boland, to Humphrey Bogart, and to Raymond Guion." (The last named later changed his name to Gene Raymond.) They settled down to a long and profitable run.

The next year Humphrey, more or less against his wishes, entered into the first of his marriages. Helen Menken, an actress of great talent and a long list of credits, fell in love with him and began a relentless pursuit. She had been on the stage since 1906, when she played one of the fairies in *A Midsummer Night's Dream*; she had played with such stars as DeWolf Hopper and John

Drew, and she had scored personal triumphs in *Three Wise Fools* and *Seventh Heaven*. She was a platinum-plated celebrity, and while she was probably ten years older than she pretended to be, she was slim and willowy and — in the fashion of the time — good-looking. The only problem was that Humphrey wasn't in love with her. One night, sitting around young Bill Brady's apartment in Turtle Bay, the subject of Helen came up and he said, "God, I don't want to marry that girl."

Stuart Rose, who was there, remembers that Brady said, "If you don't, Humphrey, you'll never get another part on Broadway."

It isn't likely that Brady meant it quite that way; the more charitable interpretation is that he meant it would be a great help for a young man on his way up to be married to an established star, but whatever his intention he succeeded in planting a small seed in Humphrey's mind. Gradually the resistance crumbled, and on May 20, 1926, Humphrey and Helen Menken were married in her apartment at the Gramercy Park Hotel.

Rose, who had married Pat Bogart two years earlier, was best man. Because of Helen's status as a celebrity there were a hundred and twenty-six guests jammed into the apartment — a sizable chunk of *Who's Who in the Theatre* — and because of the fact that both her parents were deaf-mutes, the ceremony had to be conducted in sign language. The minister was a deaf-mute who had learned to talk, like Helen Keller, and Rose's memory of the ceremony is that it was almost obscene, with the Episcopal service spoken in warped gutterals and accompanied by hand signals. The press was there, and when, after the service, Helen was supposed to meet them for a brief interview, she flew into hysterics and refused to be seen. Rose took her to an adjoining room and tried to quiet her down, but it was a long time — to him, it seemed like most of the afternoon — before she was calm enough to be interviewed. It was an ominous start for any marriage, let alone one with such a tentative bridegroom.

Trouble developed fairly soon, and before long it was clear the whole thing had been a ghastly mistake. Divorce proceedings were started in 1927, and a glimpse of Humphrey's side of it is shown in a letter he wrote his friend Lyman Brown, of the Chamberlain & Lyman Brown Theatrical Agency. He started out by saying, "By this time you have probably read in the papers about what an old meany I am," and then went on, "I have tried my very best to keep my mouth shut — and be discreet. Any talking has come from my so-called 'friends' and not from me. Do you suppose the publicity and the divorce will hurt me in a business way — I've tried to do the whole thing as nicely as possible and I don't see why it should, but I want your opinion." He ended: "When the whole thing is over Helen and I will be good friends — anyway I hope so. She tells me Chamberlain is handling all her business — I hope so because she certainly needs a manager —" Then, in crabbed writing as an afterthought, he squeezed in: "She's a wonderful girl, Lyman."

The divorce went through as scheduled, and Helen sailed to London, to repeat her success in *Seventh Heaven*.

Cradle Snatchers had closed by this time, and the only play Humphrey did in 1927 was a revival of a thing called *Baby Mine*, which Brady had once owned and which starred Fatty Arbuckle as the principal come-on. The play had first been produced in 1910 and was revived periodically thereafter, and it did nothing for either Humphrey's or Arbuckle's career. (Arbuckle's had effectively ended in 1921, with the death of one Virginia Rappe at a San Francisco hotel party, and for the next twelve years he tried unsuccessfully to get the public back on his side. Everything he touched was disaster.) But it did keep Humphrey working, which in the circumstances was a good idea. A veteran actor had once advised him that the only way to learn the trade was to work at it — and keep working, no matter how good or bad the parts might be — and he took the message to heart. It became so much a part of his life that, during his terminal illness, he fully believed he'd be all right if only he could get back to work again.

The next year he was in only one play, but this one was *Saturday's Children*, by Maxwell Anderson, and both it and he were splendid. It had opened the previous year, and he went in as a replacement. Also in April of 1928 he married Mary Philips, the actress he'd met five years before, and from all

39

points of view this was a better match than the first one. This time, the only person against the marriage was Kenneth MacKenna, who was in love with Mary himself and who would have to wait more than nine years before she once again was free. One report is that he whispered to her as she went up the aisle, "Don't marry him — marry me!" but this could be one of those things that has grown up in people's imaginations. Weddings are hectic times at best, and the witnesses aren't always reliable. Mary, who should know, points out that there was no aisle; they were married by a justice of the peace in Hartford, Connecticut, and Kenneth was nowhere about.

Humphrey and Mary had acted together in *Nerves*, and they played husband and wife the year after their marriage in a vehicle called *The Skyrocket*, which was a predictable rags-to-riches-and-back-again affair (couple happy when broke; strike it rich and are miserable; only find true love when broke again). The play was panned, but both Humphrey and Mary received warm notices. Percy Hammond, writing in the *Tribune*, said that "good actors did the best they could in the circumstances, but despite their exertions 'The Skyrocket' seemed a showy counterfeit, meaning well at heart, perhaps, but spurious upon the surface."

That was in January. In August he opened in *It's a Wise Child*, which would be his last play for two years; the Hollywood bug had begun to nibble, and from then on he spent more and more time — although at first not happily — on the West Coast.

His first picture was a ten-minute short for the Warner Brothers' Vitaphone Corporation. It was called *Broadway's Like That*, and it included Ruth Etting and Joan Blondell; Humphrey played a city slicker on the make for Miss Etting, thereby giving her a chance to sing a song. It was little noticed and quickly forgotten, and only came to light again in 1963, during research for

Mary Philips, Humphrey's second wife, in *The House Beautiful*. It was of this
play, although with no disrespect to Mary, that Dorothy Parker wrote:
"*The House Beautiful* is the play lousy."

Humphrey and Mildred McCoy in *It's a Wise Child*. Considering his expression, it's hard to see what she's laughing at.

Humphrey and Marie Wilson, in what one can only hope is a bit of deliberate clowning.

a television production. It was a technical first, and that's about all that can be said about it.

In 1930, Stuart Rose was Eastern Story Editor at Fox, working out of their New York office. It was at the time of transition from silent pictures to sound, and the studios were all frantically looking for actors and actresses who could talk. (Silent stars like John Gilbert vanished when it turned out that their voices recorded poorly.) Fox was looking for a leading man for a picture called *The Man Who Came Back*, and Rose suggested to Al Lewis, his boss, that they give Humphrey a screen test. Lewis had been a Broadway producer, of the firm of Lewis and Gordon, and his reply was to tell Rose he was out of his depth. But Rose persisted, spelling out Humphrey's various credits, and finally, more or less in desperation, they arranged for a test. A day or so later Lewis called Rose and told him to get a cab and come to the studio on Tenth Avenue; the test, he said, was "magnificent." Humphrey was hired, at seven hundred and fifty dollars a week with options, a big jump from what he'd been getting on Broadway.

Hollywood, in the 1930s, was the magic land that for millions of people symbolized success. To be called by Hollywood was to be tapped by the goddess of fame and fortune, and hordes of youths, frustrated by the Depression, made their way to California and all but flung themselves under the wheels of the movie producers' limousines in order to attract attention. Probably at no other time has so little talent been concentrated in one place, and the movie moguls wallowed in the publicity and the apparently endless source of beauty and near-beauty eager for peonage. There were all sorts of gimmicks, such as Wampus Baby Stars and the Society Starlets (one of whom, now well married, was heard to complain that "I seem to have the reputation out here of being an easy lay, and I can't understand why because I know so few people") and every now and then, perhaps once in a thousand times, there was someone who turned out to be a competent performer.

In this morass of aspiring talent it was only natural that an actor with stage experience should have a slight edge, although there is a great difference between acting before the camera and acting before a live audience. For a live audience the actor must first know all his lines, from his entrance to his final exit, and just as importantly he must speak them with enough projection so that they may be heard in the second balcony, and with gestures and facial expressions that will supplement their meaning. Before a camera, the actor needs to know only those lines in the scene about to be shot, and he needs only to *think* his mood and the camera will pick it up. Patricia Collinge, who scored a success in the stage version of *The Little Foxes*, found that she had to relearn her entire part for the movie version. She said that raising an eyebrow in front of the camera was like slamming open a window onstage, and everything that she had learned about reaching the second balcony had to be brought down and muted for the camera and the microphone. (Sir Laurence Olivier neglected this fundamental rule in his filming of *Othello*, with the result that it was badly overacted and scarcely intelligible.) To watch Gary Cooper before the camera an untrained observer would think that he was merely sitting there, possibly trying to think of his next line, but seeing the same scene in the projection room it became clear that the camera had picked up his thoughts, which spoke more than several pages of dialogue.

What helped Humphrey more than his stage experience, or anything else that he brought with him to Hollywood, was the simple fact that he was a professional. From the time, after *Swifty*, that he decided to be an actor, he devoted himself to learning his business, and he did it with a professional, no-nonsense approach that made his eventual success all but inevitable. By definition a professional is someone who is paid for doing whatever it is he does, but in the narrower sense a professional is a man who respects his trade, tries as hard as he can to perfect his work, and realizes that one failure isn't necessarily the end of the world. Or two failures. Or three. Humphrey was the very essence of this kind of professional, as even his detractors are the first to admit. There are some who don't buy the mystique that has built up around him, and there are some who claim that his acting was more a trick and a manipulation of his voice, but there are none who will try to say that he wasn't a professional.

The respect for one's trade is tied closely to, if not indistinguishable from, self-respect, and here again Humphrey was firm almost to the point of single-mindedness. He didn't always do things he was proud of — far from it — but his lapses were most usually caused by frustration, and the desire to rebel against a system that can be as frustrating as anything ever imposed on man or beast. The movie business is just that — a business — and it is run by businessmen for whom the dollar is first and art a poor second. (One of the strangest shibboleths of American life is that a businessman can fix anything, no matter what. Considering the present state of business it seems amazing that anyone could believe this, but the myth remains that a man with "good business sense" can rescue a dying venture of any sort. If a railroad is in trouble they get a board of businessmen to take over from the railroad men, and usually within a year the railroad is bankrupt. If a newspaper or a magazine is in trouble, the business board puts one of its own men at the top, and the job of editing is done by a man whose primary interest is getting more money in the till. The list of newspapers and magazines that have folded in recent years cannot be wholly blamed on the competition from television, which of course is another business; a good share of the blame can go to the fact that the men who should have been in charge were replaced by men who shouldn't.) All this holds doubly true in the movie business; a film may be cheered by the critics, but unless it makes back its production cost and more it is declared a bomb, and the man who made it will have trouble getting a second try. Conversely, a man who turns out a piece of garbage that makes money will be given *carte blanche* to do what he wants with his next picture. In the mid-fifties, when television first became a serious threat to the movies, the then head of Metro-Goldwyn-Mayer announced at a luncheon of producers, directors, and writers that henceforth no picture would be made unless it was taken from a property that was a proven success; all pictures would be written faster, shot faster, and edited faster than ever before — and all at no expense in quality. The silence that followed this announcement might just as easily have been hysterical laughter; his listeners could see the demise of the studio, like Banquo's ghost, hovering over the table.

In an atmosphere such as this a man with any self-respect is in for a long and difficult struggle, and the stiff upper lip is often hard to maintain. Humphrey was strong, but he wasn't Superman. What saved him was that he was a professional. In the eighty-one pictures that he made (some of which were shorts, or specials in which he appeared briefly) he was never late on the set, he always had his lines, and he would rehearse a scene as long as was required for the other actors to get theirs. In this last he was different from Frank Sinatra, who always gave a letter-perfect performance but would never rehearse, and Humphrey felt quite strongly that such conduct — no matter what the results — was unprofessional. In his lexicon the word *professional* was the highest praise you could give a man, but it was also the only praise; if a man was not a professional, then the hell with him. He and Sinatra were close friends, because as a singer Sinatra was in every sense a professional, but Humphrey felt that it was demeaning to the art of acting to treat it as lightly as Sinatra did. He felt that a man should try to be a professional in everything that he did.

Naturally, he didn't get the lead in *The Man Who Came Back*. He went out to Hollywood all primed for the part, and found that Fox had given the leads to Charles Farrell and Janet Gaynor, a team that had made the company a great deal of money during the silent days. (As a romantic team they were fine; off camera they looked like Mutt and Jeff. Miss Gaynor was barely five feet tall while Farrell stood about six and a half, and some tricky camera work was required to make them seem a plausible pair.) Humphrey's job was to teach Farrell how to talk, a task that turned out to be more than he was prepared to handle.

His career at Fox was not boosted by what happened one day on the golf course, when he and a friend found themselves behind a particularly slow foursome. Humphrey asked if they could play through, and one of the foursome snarled back that they certainly could not, and who the hell did he think he was to ask such a thing.

"I'm nobody," Humphrey replied. "My name is Humphrey Bogart; I work at Fox, and what are you doing playing a gentleman's game at a gentleman's club?"

When the introductions were completed, it turned out that the other man was the first vice-president at Fox.

An early publicity shot, with a caption bearing the murky message: "The rolla Boys on the Court — Kenneth MacKenna and Humphrey Bogart, featured players at the Fox Film Corporation West Coast studios, are now four-letter men, having won their letters for playing squash handball in the inter-city tournament recently held at the Hollywood A.C."

In all, he made six pictures on that first tour of duty, five for Fox and one on loan to Universal. The first one, for the record, was *A Devil with Women*, starring Victor McLaglen, and the next a dreadful comedy-melodrama called *Up the River*, with another newcomer to the screen named Spencer Tracy. (That started a friendship that lasted as long as they lived.) Humphrey played, successively, a rich playboy, an innocent convict, an aviator with weak morals, a city slicker, a decorative Marine, and a jealous ranch foreman. The length and importance of the parts deteriorated steadily, and after *A Holy Terror*, the last one, he threw up his hands and returned to New York.

A lot of things were changing at that time. The Depression had begun, unemployment was mounting, and people no longer had money to throw around as they used to. The Bogart family fortune had vanished; Dr. Bogart's health and his practice were on a downhill slide, and they moved from the West Side to an apartment in a converted brownstone at 79 East 56th Street. Apparently, it was only Mrs. Bogart's artwork that held things together at all. And in 1930 Pat Bogart Rose had gone through a twenty-seven-hour delivery, an ordeal that left her permanently unbalanced. She became a victim of manic depression, requiring periodic and increasingly frequent hospitalization. Five years later, at her insistence, Rose obtained a divorce and she was transferred to the West Coast, where Humphrey took charge. His other sister, Kay, was a beautiful girl who became a model at Bergdorf Goodman's; her only real problem was a fondness for Scotch. (George Oppenheimer, the young cofounder of Viking Press, used to call on her, and found himself unable to keep up the pace. As Humphrey said, "The trouble with George is that he gives out just as Kay's ready to give in.") Kay subsequently died of peritonitis, following a ruptured appendix.

With Hollywood, as he thought, permanently behind him, Humphrey plunged back into the theater. It was, to continue the metaphor, a dry dive. The play was *After All*, a comedy about British home life by John Van Druten, produced by Dwight Deere Wiman and starring Helen Haye (*sic*), and it opened December 3, 1931. In those days, when New York had seven newspapers, a playgoer had a wide variety of opinions to choose from, as witness this sampling from the reviews of *After All*:

". . . a pensive though not despondent comedy" — Percy Hammond, *Herald Tribune*;

". . . takes an unaccountable time to prove a truth that is obvious" — Brooks Atkinson, *Times*;

". . . if it were better played by Walter Kingsford, Humphrey Bogart, and some of the others 'After All' might have been faked into seeming more real than it is" — John Mason Brown, *Post*;

". . . a brilliant and provocative play" — Robert Garland, *World-Telegram*

In spite of being belted by the *Times* the play survived (something that would not be possible today), but Humphrey did not stay out the full run. Early in 1932 Columbia signed him to a six-month contract, and he found himself on the Santa Fe *Chief*, headed West again. One of the many phenomena about Hollywood is that people who have tried it once and hated it still find themselves going back, mumbling that maybe things will be different this time; sometimes they go back three or four times before they are finally enmeshed in it or, like a reformed drunkard, give it up for good.

The picture Columbia wanted him for was called *Love Affair*. It was based on a story by Ursula Parrott in *College Humor*, and it involved triangles within triangles and misunderstandings and love affairs and a certain amount of flying. Its main benefit for Humphrey was that it gave him second lead to Dorothy Mackaill, one of the more popular young actresses of the time, and this could have been a springboard to bigger and better parts. But then

Columbia loaned him out to Warners for a thing called *Big City Blues*, starring Joan Blondell, in which he received tenth billing, and the only thing it got him was a chance to flatten Lyle Talbot, who was billed sixth. One more picture for Warners, called *Three on a Match*, and he was ready to return to New York. The only things *Three on a Match* offered him were slightly better billing (sixth) and a chance to play something different from his usual pretty-boy roles. He played a character called The Mug, a hired kidnapper who is foiled when Ann Dvorak jumps out a window with a message in lipstick on her nightgown. (Never mind the details; an explanation would only confuse things further.)

So back he came to the theater, and to life in New York in the Depression. It is the general consensus that it was Mary who supported them during the bleaker periods; her reputation was such that she was seldom without work, and she was an equalizing factor during his occasional moments of irresponsibility. Edith Oliver, now off-Broadway drama critic for *The New Yorker*, was working at the Berkshire Playhouse in Stockbridge in 1932, when Mary was playing in stock there, and Humphrey, freshly back from Hollywood, came up to visit. He was drunk a good deal of the time but he was charming, and he entertained the company with hilarious stories about Hollywood. Mary's only reaction was an offhand remark that she had never understood Carry Nation before, but was now beginning to. In spite of the drinking, Miss Oliver was enchanted by him; she says simply that "Bogart had class — he was such a gent!" This in the circumstances is a remarkable reaction, and it may be a sign of one of those qualities that were later to make him a star.

On the other hand, it could just be the contrast between Humphrey and the senior Brady, who was also at Stockbridge and also drunk. Katherine Alexander, young Bill's wife, was in a play that was trying out, and the old man's reactions from across the footlights were loud, continuous, and profane. In Act III George Coulouris made his entrance, and Brady shouted, "Well, *that's* the first two-balled man in the whole goddam cast!" Compared to Brady, a whistling marmoset would have seemed a gentleman. (As a footnote to Brady's personality: For twelve weeks during 1917, his press agent was a Puritanical, nondrinking, would-be writer named Robert C. Benchley; the arrangement collapsed when the employee's obvious distaste for the employer's way of life made further collaboration impossible. Brady was "not prostrated" by the younger man's departure.)

Whatever Humphrey's behavior at Stockbridge, there is nobody from this period who remembers him as anything but a gentleman. There are still those who insist he never changed; that even at his most rambunctious his innate politeness never left him. This is open to documentary refutation, as is their theory that he never used foul language, but there was apparently some streak within him, some imp that was loosed by a variety of factors, which brought out the atypical. He was, at heart, a Puritan; he despised dirty stories, and anyone who told one — especially if there were women present — was rewarded with a pained smirk, and total silence. His moral code was strict, and was based on and almost indistinguishable from the Ten Commandments; although he had four wives there were never any girls on the sidelines, and in a community where infidelity was taken for granted and promiscuity was cheered, he was only slightly behind Judge Hardy as far as fidelity was concerned. In that category, he had Lassie lashed to the mast.

The life of a young actor in New York during the Depression was a thin one. Humphrey and Mary lived in an apartment at 434 East 52nd Street, and their main recreation was playing bridge or Parcheesi or Monopoly or whatnot with friends. Under the "whatnot" heading was a certain amount of pub-crawling, but nobody could afford very much of that, and the speakeasy liquor made it a toss-up as to who ended up blind, paralyzed, or dead. (Needled beer, which was near-beer spiked with ether, could blind you, and at one point the government deliberately distributed poisoned liquor in an attempt to frighten people away from drinking. Like some other government undercover work, it boomeranged. The safest thing was to make your own.) In everything he did, Humphrey was careful to the point of being meticulous. Nothing was sloppy, even the way he held his cigarette, and people still remember the painstaking way he counted out the moves on a Parcheesi board. They'd say, "Humphrey, it's ten from there to here," but still he'd count, touching each space of the ten. He was a careful player in everything including sports, and a money player when it came to stakes. The only recorded time that he brought levity into a game was once when he and Mary were playing bridge with Miriam Howell and her husband Ralph Warren, and he produced a revolver, slapped it on the table, and said, "Now let's play bridge." The Warrens were too rattled to appreciate the joke.

But of all the games, chess was his favorite. He learned it from his father, and it became what amounted to a lifelong addiction. At one point in New York, he and Mary lived near one of those storefront arrangements where they had a dozen chess boards set up, and you won a dollar if you beat the expert; Humphrey beat the expert so often that he was offered the job as expert, but he turned it down. He was making more money by winning as an outsider. He would play chess with anyone who offered; he'd play it in person, by telephone, or by mail, and during idle moments he'd work out chess problems by himself, just to keep in shape. Students of the film *Casablanca* will recall that the first shot of Rick shows him playing solitary chess; this was a touch of Humphrey's, to give him something to do as the scene opened. (Actors have a built-in aversion to simply sitting there and reading lines, and they are forever looking for an angle, or a mood, or an approach with which to start a scene.) Coincidentally, he believed that concentration was the most important element in acting, and the concentration required in chess was one and the same thing. By sharpening his chess, he was, so to speak, exercising his acting muscle.

On December 5, 1933, the repeal of the Eighteenth Amendment went into effect, and all those who'd been drinking speakeasy liquor and making bathtub gin made plans for a glorious binge, or bender, or toot, to use a few of the then current terms. The Bogarts and Melvin and Mary Baker (he a writer, she an agent) decided that the whole thing should be done with great class — "a white thigh and tails evening," as they put it — and they would dress to the teeth and go only to the best places. They went first to the Ritz bar, where they had a few cocktails in the elegant atmosphere, and then, as they were starting for the Waldorf for dinner, it was discovered that Humphrey had a button missing from his Chesterfield. Deeply embarrassed, he took his plight to one of the barmen, who went off into the hotel, located a button, and sewed it on for him. Once more resplendent they trooped off to the Waldorf, and here the memories of the two survivors differ. Mary Baker says that the Waldorf had not yet received its liquor license; Mary MacKenna says that they simply hadn't made reservations — whatever the reason, their planned gala fell through and they wound up the evening at Tony's, a speakeasy they'd been going to for years.

The first play Humphrey went into on his return from Hollywood was *I Loved You Wednesday*, a brittle comedy that opened and closed in October of 1932. He played a character named Randall Williams, "a sybarite with the morals of a tom-cat," and while John Mason Brown wrote that "Humphrey Bogart makes the bounder-architect as attractive as the text demands," that wasn't enough. The only other item of interest about the play was that a young man named Henry Fonda was also in the cast.

A month later he opened in the Theatre Guild production of *Chrysalis*, and again he was cast as a bounder, but by now the critics were beginning to weary of the typecasting. Atkinson kissed him off by saying that "Bogart plays the wastrel in his usual style," but Hammond went into more incisive detail: "Mr. Bogart, an oily insect, gets Miss [Margaret] Sullivan drunk and instructs her, through many long and monotonous kisses, in what he refers to as 'the joys of propinquity.' " As for the play, Atkinson found it "astonishingly insignificant," Hammond said the production was "awkward and nit-wit," Lockridge also panned it, and only Garland, the *World-Telegram*'s resident Pollyanna, stood up for it. "One of the meaningful, beautiful things this season has brought," he wrote.

What was happening, although Humphrey probably wouldn't have admitted it, was that he was becoming an aging juvenile, which is one of the most deadly categories there is. The actor who can't break out of it is doomed, because makeup can conceal only just so much, and after a while his voice begins to give him away. Add to that the *ennui* of the critics and the public, and he might as well look for a new line of work. (Symptomatic of this was the fed-up moviegoer who, many years ago, vowed not to see another Mickey Rooney picture until they filmed *Death Comes to Andy Hardy*.)

54

It was probably just as well that Humphrey received no notices at all in his next play, which was *The Mask and the Face*, translated by W. Somerset Maugham from the Italian of Luigi Chiarelli, and which was characterized by such epithets as "a grisly farce," "a tepid comedy," and "a dubious graveyard lark." It was at least a change of pace, but that was about all that could be said for it.

He then made a picture, *Midnight*, which was shot in New York for Universal and in which he played a gangster, another change of pace except that he was a romantic gangster, with very little to do except get killed by his girl friend in a fit of pique. The part could have been played by a trained bear, and he regretted the time he'd taken to do it. As far as he was concerned, he and motion pictures were finished — unless something really important came along.

In May of 1934 he opened in a play that, while it didn't seem so at the time, was the beginning of a turning point in his life. It was an old-fashioned mystery melodrama by Rufus King, titled *Invitation to a Murder*, and it was complete with trapdoors, ghosts, and all the clichés of the clutching-hand school of drama. Humphrey played Horatio Channing, a member of a southern California family whose fortune was founded on piracy, and even old Pollyanna Garland stifled a yawn as he wrote that "Humphrey Bogart Humphrey-Bogarts his way through the role." The *Post* summed it up as "high-voltage trash," and it might have been just another step toward oblivion if Arthur Hopkins, a producer-director, hadn't seen it and remembered Humphrey's performance when he was casting a new play. The play was Robert E. Sherwood's *The Petrified Forest*, and Hopkins asked Humphrey to read for a part. Wondering what new kind of pretty-boy role he was going to be assigned, Humphrey went around to the office in the Plymouth Theatre, and when Hopkins said he wanted him to read Duke Mantee, the escaped killer, both Humphrey and Sherwood were flabbergasted. Sherwood and Hopkins argued back and forth, Sherwood maintaining that the role of Boze Hertzlinger, the ex-football player, was more in Humphrey's line, and Humphrey, while he didn't interfere, silently agreed. It was the kind of part he could play with his eyes closed, the self-satisfied Lothario who is forever nuzzling the heroine and trying to get her out into the mesquite, and he thought Hopkins must be crazy to want him for the gangster. But hungry actors have no choice, and when Sherwood finally gave in and said he'd listen, Humphrey figured the least he could do was give it a try. And that was all that was needed.

W HEN HUMPHREY WALKED ONSTAGE as Duke Mantee there was a stir in the audience, an audible intake of breath. He *was* a criminal; he walked with a convict's shuffling gait, and his hands dangled in front of him as though held there by the memory of manacles. His voice was flat and his eyes were as cold as a snake's; he bore an eerie resemblance to John Dillinger, to whom killing a person meant no more than breaking a matchstick. Sherwood's summary of Mantee in the stage directions described Bogart perfectly: "He is well-built but stoop-shouldered, with a vaguely thoughtful, saturnine face. He is about thirty-five and, if he hadn't elected to take up banditry, he might have been a fine leftfielder. There is, about him, one quality of resemblance to Alan Squier [the hero]: he too is unmistakably doomed."

The play opened at the Broadhurst Theatre on January 7, 1935, with Leslie Howard starring as Alan Squier and Peggy Conklin as Gabrielle Maple, the heroine. (For those interested in trivia, the part of Boze Hertzlinger, which had almost been Humphrey's, was played by a youth named Frank Milan.) The story, briefly, tells how Squier, a wandering intellectual, meets and befriends Gabrielle in an Arizona roadhouse, and sees in her some of the dreams he had once had as a youth. Mantee, fleeing the police, comes on the scene as the incarnation of ruthless violence, and makes hostages of everyone in the roadhouse. Squier signs over his life insurance to Gabrielle and then gets Mantee to shoot him, so that Gabrielle can have the money to go back to her mother's homeland in France. That is overcompression of the most radical

DRAWING BY FRUEH, COPYRIGHT 1935, 1963 THE NEW YORKER MAGAZINE, INC.

"THE PETRIFIED FOREST"

Leslie Howard may seem a bit lackadaisical here, but it is because he is concentrating on Life and Miss Peggy Conklin, leaving the action to Humphrey Bogart in the background.

A *New Yorker* cartoon about *The Petrified Forest*.

sort, but any explanation short of printing the entire script would be of little help.

The critics threw their hats in the air. Brooks Atkinson wrote that "Robert Sherwood's new play is a peach . . . a roaring Western melodrama . . . Humphrey Bogart does the best work of his career as the motorized guerilla," and Robert Garland said that "Humphrey Bogart is gangster Mantee to the tip of his sawed-off shotgun." The play, clearly, was in for a long run.

Humphrey had had one bad period in September, before rehearsals started, when his father died. Things had been getting progressively worse; Dr. and Mrs. Bogart had moved to Tudor City, and with the almost complete disappearance of his practice, he had taken up the periodic job of ship's doctor on cruise ships or small passenger liners. He died in the Hospital for the Ruptured and Crippled in New York, leaving approximately ten thousand dollars in debts, which Humphrey paid off out of his eventual earnings from *The Petrified Forest*. Humphrey had a deep affection for his father, and his death at this time, and in these circumstances, was a particularly jarring blow.

But once rehearsals were under way, he put everything else behind him and concentrated on becoming as convincing a gangster as possible. He walked, talked, and lived Duke Mantee; he wore a felt hat with the brim turned down, he talked out of the side of his mouth, and he built up a set of mannerisms to go with the character. There are very few shows that don't have some sort of trouble or conflict prior to (and sometimes after) opening night, but Hopkins had chosen his cast well. A short, round, brown, slightly bowlegged little man, he quietly mesmerized the actors into doing what he wanted, and since in many instances he had intuitively cast them against type (as in Bogart's case) the results were often electric. He told them that he collected casts the way other people collect books, and that this was the perfect cast; there was not one person in it he'd think of changing.

Another case of the intuitive casting was that of Ester Leeming, who played a small part as Paula, a Mexican cook. When Hopkins picked her (a simple nod was his usual method of selection) Sherwood said to her, "It's lucky you

The new Bogart, in the film version of *The Petrified Forest*. It was an image that would follow him the rest of his life.

The Petrified Forest. With Charlie
Grapewin, Bette Davis, Leslie Howard,
and Dick Foran.

can speak Spanish. The only Spanish I know is 'patio,' and I learned that in Hollywood." As it turned out she couldn't speak Spanish, so she went to Berlitz and took a cram course until she could swear convincingly in the language — which she still can do to this day.

Their first night in front of an audience was in mid-December at the Parsons Theatre in Hartford, and there were two things that astonished the company. One was the amount of humor in the script — lines took on a new meaning, which they'd missed in rehearsal — and the other was the literal gasp that went up when Humphrey made his entrance. Dillinger was very much in the news at the time, having recently escaped from prison, and to some people it seemed that he had just walked onstage. The prison pallor, the two-days' beard, the gait, the mannerisms — everything about him was menacing, evil, and real. The company was to hear that gasp every night throughout the run, but the first one was the one they still remember. They went on to Boston, where they opened Christmas Eve, and then to New York in January. They played until June 29 of that year.

For two reasons, Humphrey disdained the use of makeup. The first was that the desired effect of prison pallor made makeup unnecessary, and the second was that to fake a two-days' beard would be obvious. His was his real beard, and he kept it trimmed during the week with electric clippers, thereby becoming one of the earlier electric shavers. After the Saturday night performance he would shave, singing and lathering himself and having a grand old time, and he would come into Miss Leeming's dressing room, which adjoined his, and spread his good cheer around with a lavish hand. She remembers him as being generally quiet and gentle, and scrupulous in his behavior to the female members of the cast — a trait that was by no means shared by the star.

The play could have run for a much longer time, but Howard grew weary of playing it. He had enough muscle with the producers (he was a coproducer with Gilbert Miller, in association with Hopkins) so that he could forbid anyone else to take his part, and also to prevent its going on the road. Warners had by this time bought it, and Howard announced that a road tour might hurt the box office for the picture. So they closed the end of June, while still doing booming business; Howard went home to England, and the others went looking for jobs. One of those who felt the disappointment most keenly was Howard's understudy, Kenneth MacKenna.

One of the good things Howard did, however, was to say that he would do the picture only if Bogart played Mantee, and he was as good as his word. Warners had Edward G. Robinson under contract, and saw no sense in using someone they'd already had a few unspectacular dealings with, so they blithely announced they were making the picture with Howard and Robinson, and with Bette Davis playing Gabrielle. Humphrey, understandably upset, cabled the news to Howard, and Howard cabled Warners that without Bogart he wouldn't play. They gave in, and Humphrey was signed to another Warners Brothers contract. His farewell to the stage was a summer of stock in Skowhegan, Maine, where he did such plays as *Rain* and *Ceiling Zero* while waiting for the shooting to begin on *The Petrified Forest*. He was a quick study and a perfectionist and he had each part letter-perfect, playing one while rehearsing another.

The film version of Sherwood's play was remarkably similar to the original, with only a few obligatory outdoor shots and some tinkering with the dialogue to make the difference. (In the play, Gabrielle tells Squier: "My name is Gabrielle, but these ignorant bastards call me Gabby," a line which until recently would never be allowed on screen.) The screenplay was by Charles Kenyon and Delmer Davis and the director was Archie Mayo; of the original company, only Bogart and Howard and one minor player remained.

In Hollywood it is a truism that a person is as good as his last screen credit, and having scored as a gangster Humphrey was immediately cast as another. The picture was *Bullets or Ballots* and Humphrey played a character named Nick "Bugs" Fenner, who in the last reel kills and is killed by a hard-boiled sleuth, played by Edward G. Robinson. In his first two years at Warners he made twelve pictures, in eight of which he was either a gangster or a criminal of some sort, and in four of which he was killed. In one he was sent to prison for life, and in one other he and Robinson repeated their double-killing routine. Exactly two, *Marked Woman* (with Bette Davis) and *Dead End*, were what might be called superior pictures, and one, *Isle of Fury*, was so bad that he pretended not to remember ever having made it. In it he wore a pencil-line moustache, and looked something like Errol Flynn.

When he and Mary had gone to Hollywood in 1930 they stayed at a place called Hollywoodland; in 1936 they went first to the Chateau Elysee and then to the Garden of Allah, a collection of bungalows surrounding a pool and adjoining a main building, once the home of the actress Alla Nazimova. (The pool was shaped like the Black Sea, the area from which Nazimova had come, and the name was a feeble pun on hers.) In the 1930s the Garden of Allah was famous for its transient population: writers, actors, and celebrities of various shapes and sizes made it their headquarters, and their carryings-on were reported by the Sunday-supplement writers for the delectation of an eager public. It survived into the 1960s, going gradually downhill, and when finally it was razed and an office building constructed in its place on Sunset Boulevard, a lot was written about The Good Old Days and the Glamour of Old Hollywood. Glamour is a slippery quality, consisting mostly of imagination, but the Garden did have an atmosphere all its own. Perhaps it was the propinquity of the bungalows, some so close together that a tenant once got up in the middle of the night, heeding a lady's request for water, and didn't find out until he returned to the unoccupied bed that the voice had come from next door. Or it could have been the lush foliage, so thick that another tenant, awakened by a large bird outside his window, was able to rush out and give the bird a roundhouse right to the beak before it could extricate itself and fly off. It could have been any number of reasons or a combination of them all; whatever the cause, the Garden of Allah was The Place to Stay when you were in Hollywood.

But it now looked as though Humphrey was there for good, so he and Mary began to look for something not for transients. They took a small adobe house on Horn Avenue, a street that rises steeply into the hills north of Sunset Boulevard, the downhill end terminating almost in the door of the Utter-McKinley funeral parlor. Utter-McKinley advertised on benches at bus stops, and their display ad, so to speak, was a large clock on the side of the building with a swinging pendulum — and no hands. It was Humphrey's fervent hope

66

58047

that someday a car would roll down Horn Avenue and crash into the building, and to that end he avoided warning guests that they should park with their wheels cocked against the curb. The ploy didn't work, but Utter-McKinley was reputedly involved in another kind of accident: one night wags painted hands on the clock, and there was a fatal crash at that intersection at precisely the time indicated by the hands. That, at any rate, is the legend. The Utter-McKinley clock is no longer there.

There was one big drawback to the whole scene: Mary was a stage and not a motion-picture actress, and she continued to return to the East to appear in plays. She had her own career, which had kept them going during the leaner years, and she saw no reason why she shouldn't continue it. Humphrey, on the other hand, felt that now he was able to support them both she should stay with him, and he was faintly irritated when she left to do something on her own. In the circumstances he was wide open for trouble, and he found it. Her name was Mayo Methot, who in her earlier years had been named "The Portland Rosebud," and she was a short, chunky blond with a mean left hook and a fondness for Scotch. He met her at the home of the writer Eric Hatch and his wife, who lived on Beverly Drive, and he continued to meet her there while the Hatches watched nervously from the sidelines. Mayo was a sometime actress, and she appeared in a small role in *Marked Woman*, and by the time Mary returned from New York it was apparent that her and Humphrey's marriage was over.

Mary Baker, his friend from the white-thigh-and-tails evening and also his agent, recalls that her impression was he really didn't want to marry Mayo; that he'd been trapped in a situation and didn't know how to get out. She saw him on the set of *Dead End*, glumly practicing throwing a penknife at an orange peel (a trick that William Wyler, the director, had asked him to perfect before going on camera), and while he flipped the knife at the orange peel they discussed his problem. Finally, and wearily, he said, "I guess that means I'll have to marry Mayo," and with that the machinery was set in motion, but it was done with no more enthusiasm than his first marriage. Like Helen Menken, Mayo had been determined to get him, and like Helen Menken she succeeded for a while.

67

And here we have an odd picture: the hairy-chested tough guy being intimidated by women. Dime-store psychiatrists would have a field day with this; they would point to his domineering mother and his comparatively ineffectual father, and they would go on to cite his reluctant marriage to Helen Menken, a woman ten years his senior who chased him into a corner and bullied him into marrying her. They would then proceed to emphasize the fact that he was dependent on Mary Philips in the early years of their marriage, and was conned by Mayo Methot into leaving Mary for her, and that even his fourth wife, to whom he was devoted, was the one who called the shots in their domestic affairs. He was in many ways a docile husband, and your shoot-from-the-hip analysts would say that all his bluster and tough talk were a cover-up for doubts about his masculinity. They would theorize that he had fears of impotence and/or homosexuality (as a matter of fact he *did* have a brief spell of impotence, back when he was first married to Mary, but his recovery was quick and, as later events testified, complete), and they would say if he was such a he-man then how come he didn't keep a few chicks on the side, like practically everyone else in Hollywood? And how come if he was a real man he never followed through with the fights he liked to start? Speculation along this line is an oversimplification, in view of the other angles that might be explored. Consider the possibilities:

A man who has been married four times, twice more or less against his wishes, is either too much of a gentleman — or too much of a coward — to say no, or he is ambitious and hopes the marriages will advance his career, or is a satyr who can't be satisfied with one woman, or is forever looking for Mom. Those are a few of the more obvious reasons, and while some might be said to fit Bogart's case there isn't one that covers the whole business completely.

He was, for instance, a gentleman at heart. He inherited this from his father, of whom he was extremely fond and who, ineffectual or not, was a gentle man in every sense of the word, and if Bogie seemed at times to be trying his best to conceal this inheritance it was nevertheless there, and it showed up most often when least expected. It could be argued that, once he had gone to certain lengths with a woman, he considered it ungentlemanly to back out, but that is a thin argument that wouldn't stand up against much buffeting. Turning it around and saying he was too much of a coward to back out would be a much thinner case, although there were some who chose to find cowardice in much that he did.

As for the ambition theory, a case could certainly be made for that in his first marriage, when Bill Brady told him he'd never get another part if he didn't marry Helen, and when he subsequently wondered to Lyman Brown if the divorce would hurt his career, but there isn't a shred of evidence to show that any of his other marriages were based on ambition. He had known and liked Mary Philips for a long time, and if in fact it was she who provided most of the support it was not that he wasn't also working, and gaining a reputation on his own. As far as Mayo was concerned, there was nothing she could do to advance his career — in fact, it could most easily have been to the contrary.

The satyr theory is wholly inapplicable here. Sex was low on his list of hobbies, to a point where he one night became so incensed at a Los Angeles trollop that his companions had to pull him away before he did her bodily harm. Only once could anyone recall his even looking at a female other than his wife, and that was done purely as a needle. It didn't even come in the category of a pass; it was a brief flurry of attention, and it would have gone unnoticed if it hadn't been so out of character. It succeeded in its intention of irritating his spouse, and that was that. Oddly enough, he couldn't even *act* like a satyr; in a film called *Battle Circus*, in 1953, he was supposed to be a Medical Corps Major in hot pursuit of June Allyson (yes, June Allyson), and the lines he was forced to read turned to sawdust in his mouth. It can seldom be said that he gave an unconvincing performance, but nobody who had ever seen Bogart before would have been convinced by the leering gropes he made in Miss Allyson's direction. Try to imagine the Lord Olivier impersonating Shirley Temple, and you will have a rough idea of the incongruity.

As for the looking-for-Mom theory, there is no doubt that he was brought up by a strong mother, and his first marriage could have been considered a continuation of the pattern. But that marriage lasted approximately a year, and his wives thereafter were about his own age or, as in the case of the last

The start of a turbulent era: Bogie and Mayo Methot after filing notice, on
August 12, 1938, of their intention to wed.

one, twenty-five years younger. Mary Philips was strong, in that she was what might be called an anchor to windward, but she was in no way domineering, and if anyone had the upper hand in their relationship it was he, who did and said precisely as he chose. And while Mayo was many things she was by no stretch of the imagination a mother figure, unless you picture your mother wearing boxing gloves. If Bogie was looking for Mom, he was — to mix the metaphor — barking up the wrong tree on that one.

So what is the answer? The simplest and most obvious one is that he was never really in love on any of the first three occasions. He was certainly not in love with Helen; he may have been with Mary but it didn't survive the pull of their separate careers, and while he might have been fascinated by Mayo there is nothing to show that he was ever what could be called deeply in love. That didn't happen until the fourth time around, and when it did happen, that was it.

If there is a minor difference of opinion about some details of Bogart's marriage to Mary Philips, it is nothing compared to the whirlwind of conflicting reports about his marriage to Mayo Methot. Most accounts agree that it took place on August 21, 1938, that Judge Ben Lindsay performed the ceremony, and that it was held at the home of the Mel Bakers in Bel Air. There was a terraced lawn sloping away from the badminton court, where the tables were set up, and Mrs. Walter Abel is generally conceded to have been playing a harp in the shrubbery at the top of the terrace, but beyond that the survivors' accounts begin to differ. Allen Rivkin, a writer who was present, recalls that the ceremony was held at noon; people began to arrive about ten, he says, and by noon the whole party was smashed. Mary Baker, at whose house it was held, swears that it was a dinner party, with the ceremony taking place in the late afternoon. At least two people remember seeing Mischa Auer crawling naked beneath the tables, but others tend to doubt it on the theory that a thing like that wouldn't go unnoticed by the general assemblage. Those who claim to have seen it, however, are quite vivid in their recollections. It is generally accepted that at one point or another Bogie cried, because he always cried at weddings ("He cried at every one of his own weddings," Lauren Bacall said much later, adding, "And with good reason.") But the climax, as remembered by Mary Baker, was that the bride and groom had a fight, Bogie and Mel Baker went to Mexico, and she and Mayo shared the was-to-have-been wedding bed. She says that the contrite bridegroom sent a rubber plant as a peace offering next day. Others have absolutely no memory of such an event; some tend to doubt it strongly; and some simply say, "I wouldn't know." The one point on which everyone agrees is that it was a bang-up party.

Mayo was an excellent housekeeper and a devoted wife and daughter-in-law; she adored and was in return adored by Mrs. Bogart, who came often to stay with them in the new and larger house they took on Horn Avenue. Humphrey, for his part, was quite fond of Buffy Methot, Mayo's mother; she was an avid beer drinker, and he bought her cases of it for Christmas. It would have been a good marriage all around, if it hadn't been for Mayo's violent, insane jealousy, mixed equal parts with Scotch. If Bogie literally so much as looked at another woman she was likely to hit him with either her fist or the nearest weapon; she once knocked him off the dock and into Newport Harbor when she saw his eyes flick toward a girl getting out of a boat. But it didn't have to be for an immediate reason; Charles Lederer, the screenwriter, remembers an evening at Peter Lorre's house, where everyone had gone after dinner, and there was suddenly a sound like a pistol shot. Mayo had hit Bogie on the head with a large wooden spoon, while he was leaning over inspecting a collection of African artifacts.

But it wasn't only her husband who received the brunt of Mayo's rages. Tay Garnett, the writer-producer-director, was with them in "21" one night, and Mayo turned on him and said, "Why can't the best actor in the world get anything but heavy parts — and what the hell are you going to do about it?" Garnett replied that if the right part came along, he'd be happy to cast Bogart in it, and the evening wound up with Mayo throwing crockery at both of them, just on general principles. Sometime later, Garnett was casting a comedy called *Stand-In*, with Leslie Howard and Joan Blondell, and it occurred to him that the second lead was something that Bogart could play very nicely. The role was of a director who'd drunk himself out of pictures and was trying to make a comeback, and there were several comedy scenes

Bogie and Mayo aboard *Sluggy*. On the back of the picture he wrote to Eric Hatch:
"Dear Eric — Here's *Sluggy* — note house flag — we sling dinghy from davits
in stern — and now fly Coast Guard flag and are getting quite active — have
also bought a Dyer sailing dinghy in case we're grounded. Wish you'd
come out soon. Regards Bogie."

The inscription, to the Masseys, is a line from *Action in the North Atlantic:*
"Fog rolling in, Mister — Hard right and keep a sharp lookout."

with Howard, who played an efficiency expert trying to resuscitate a moribund movie company. It would, Garnett reasoned, not only get Bogart out of the rut he was in, but it might also give him a chance to play the breezy charmer and start him off toward romantic leads. He suggested this to Walter Wanger, his partner and producer of the picture, and Wanger didn't think much of it. Finally, after considerable argument, Wanger gave in and Bogart was loaned from Warners to play the part. One day while watching the rushes, Paul Schwagler, the second assistant director, looked at Garnett and said, "You're crazy if you think you'll make a hero out of him — the son of a bitch lisps!"

The main trouble was that *Stand-In* wasn't much of a picture, and his respite from gangland didn't last long. Back at Warners, he did an abysmal hillbilly comedy called *Swing Your Lady*, then two more nothing pictures in which he was the good-guy lead, and then he was back on the heavy circuit again. (One of these, *The Amazing Dr. Clitterhouse*, was a psychological confusion he scornfully referred to as "The Amazing Dr. Clitoris." The only thing worthy of note was that the coauthor of the screenplay was John Huston, who later was to have an important part in the Bogart career.) From 1938 through 1940 he made seventeen pictures, in eleven of which he was either a gangster or a criminal, and in nine of which he died. Garnett had kept his word to Mayo, but he was fighting a losing battle. The only outstanding picture during this period was *Dark Victory*, again with Bette Davis.

One of the problems with his casting was that Jack Warner didn't believe he had any romantic potential, and no matter how hard Bogart fought for better parts, Warner always had the box-office figures to buttress his defense of the gangster roles. (Box-office figures, as has been indicated, rank somewhere between the Torah and the Dead Sea Scrolls; Brackett and Wilder had to wait until Paramount analyzed their previous box-office results before they were allowed to use the lot for making *The Lost Weekend*, and even then they were warned not to tell a soul where they were making it. After the Academy Awards came out, of course, it was a different story.) Bogart complained bitterly about his casting but he seldom refused a part, and as his list of credits mounted the gangster image became overpowering. Late in

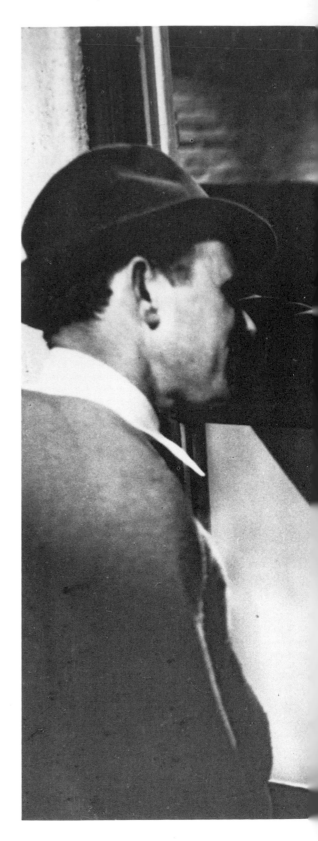

With Leslie Howard, listening to director
Tay Garnett in *Stand-In*. This was an early
— and unsuccessful — attempt to rid him
of the gangster image.

1940 he made a personal appearance at a Broadway movie house in New York, and his act started with a darkened house while one after another of his death scenes was flashed on the screen. Then the house lights came up and there he was, lying flat on his face on the stage. He rose, smiled, said, "It's a hell of a way to make a living," then dusted off his hands and went into a brief routine. It was the first time most people had seen the cheerful side of him, and the effect was startling. Hordes of people, the majority of them women, mobbed his dressing-room door, and Mary Baker put through a triumphant call to Jack Warner, announcing that his "nonromantic" actor was besieged by slavering females. Warner's reply is not recorded.

Probably the best way to illustrate his public image at that time is to reprint an interview from the *New York Herald Tribune.* It ran in the Sunday drama section on December 8, 1940, and is here reproduced with the permission of the reporter who wrote it.* The headline, written by Arthur H. Folwell, the drama editor, was "Screen Bad Man Finds His Fun Playing Bad Man Off-stage, Too." The piece follows:

A short while ago I went to interview Humphrey Bogart and at the conclusion of the more formal part of the interview he had his coat off and was chasing me and I was chasing something that later turned out to be a cat. The formal part consisted of my saying, "What am I going to write about you?" and his replying, "That's your worry." So much for unfinished business.

There was one thing I found out, however — without his telling me in so many words — and that is that these screen bad men are not necessarily heaven's own children off the screen. There has been a lot written about the fact that Mr. Bogart started his dramatic career by coming onstage with a tennis racquet and inviting some of the handsomer males off into the wings for a few sets; the handouts have insisted that he is crazy about the color brown and about gladioli, and the whole idea has been that he is a shy little mouse when he isn't in front of the camera and shooting guns at other mobsters. I know what that is a lot of.

* Copyright, *New York Herald Tribune* (I.H.T. Corporation).

Not that he should be locked up on the spot — he is a law-abiding, congenial, and, all in all, a very nice person — but the idea that he is not dangerous is one of those mistakes that should have been rectified long ago.

The trouble is, he is an actor. Not that this news will knock anyone over backward, but when he feels so inclined he will slip into one of his screen parts, just for the fun of it, with the result that the living life is frightened out of the people in his immediate vicinity.

The first time I ever saw him I was with someone who knew about this and who decided to put on a little show for the benefit of the people who were busying themselves with enjoying their dinners. He went up to the bar, and tapped Bogart on the shoulder. "All right," he said. "Finish your drink and get out of here. We don't want you in this place."

Bogart looked around, slowly and ominously took his cigarette out of his mouth and flipped it on the ground, and moved up so that their faces were eight inches apart. He squinted slightly as he spat out the last of his cigarette smoke. A waiter looked nervously at the bartender, who reached one hand under the counter.

"Listen," said Bogart, "I'm staying here, and if you don't like it you can move along. This is my territory and you know it. Or do I have to prove it to you?"

The nearest person at the bar slid back a couple of yards, his eyes popping, and a few of the other guests began nervously to get themselves behind the furniture.

The whole thing blew over when Bogart broke down and began to laugh, but I learned later that these two had on occasion come to blows, pulling their punches but pretending that they were cutting each other to ribbons.

As though this weren't enough, Bogart has a wife, Mayo Methot, an actress, who joins whole-heartedly in these little forays. And if anyone wasn't convinced at the beginning of one of these scenes, he certainly would be by the sight of a beautiful woman hysterically trying to separate the combatants and telling them that she hates the sight of two men fighting over her.

On the occasion of my so-called interview the first part of the evening passed comparatively quietly. A Washington correspondent also was on the scene, but he did nothing but request "Lover" from the pianist all evening, so there was no fight from that quarter. Finally, after all the other guests had left, a waiter gave us our check, which Bogart immediately appropriated. I do not mean to imply that I broke my arm grabbing for the check (we had been there four hours), but somehow a harsh word was passed, and in a flash Bogart stood up, dropped his coat, and lunged at me, but not before Mrs. Bogart had thrown herself between us.

"Stop it!" she pleaded. "Boys, please stop it! No . . . I can't watch . . . Bogie, don't hit him — he's young . . . for my sake don't hit him . . ."

For three horrible seconds she had me convinced. In those three seconds I remembered "The Petrified Forest," "Dead End," "Kid Galahad," and a few more such cheerful episodes, and it seemed to me perfectly possible that an actor might be influenced by the parts he played. Out of the corner of my eye I saw something small and brown, which I felt much more like fighting, go past the table, so I turned and made after it. It was only a cat, but I reasoned you can't hit a man who has a cat in his arms.

Obviously, my defensive alliance with the cat was unnecessary, but I figured that a few scratches would be better than a few fractures and internal injuries.

There is only one drawback to this little game, aside from the fright of those who are fooled by it, and that is that somewhere, some day, Bogart may play it with some person who has friends that are more loyal than discerning. There is no more dangerous man in the world than the little man who has a lot of taxi drivers for friends, since they will rally to his support with lug wrenches, spanners, and crank handles the minute they think he has even been insulted. They wouldn't wait to hear that Bogart and their friend were only playing.

But that is Bogart's worry.

Generally speaking, domestic squabbles make dismal reading and are best left unrecorded, but the Bogarts' fights were so frequent and so spectacular, and with no apparent damage to their marriage, that they deserve a brief examination. Fights of their intensity and regularity would have dissolved most marriages within a month. They were mostly started by Mayo — the violent part, at any rate — and usually when she was in her cups, but there were too many exceptions to make this hold up as a flat rule. As an example, they were awakened one morning, in their room at the Gotham Hotel in New York, by a telephone call from their writer friend Daniel Mainwaring. Mayo took the phone, then reached it over to Bogie, said, "It's for you," and dropped it in his face. He slugged her, and they leaped from the bed, stark naked, and began to throw things at each other. The skirmish went on for several minutes, and then Mayo picked up a potted plant, and as she got it above her head it overbalanced her, and she crashed heavily to the floor. Convulsed with laughter, Bogie fell back on the bed, retrieved the telephone, and said, "Yeah, Danny, what did you want?" The day then went on as though nothing had happened.

They became known as the Battling Bogarts, and things finally reached the point where Mac Kriendler, of "21," barred them as a couple from the establishment. Singly they were welcome, he said, but together they were more than any self-respecting restaurateur cared to handle. (It was not a ban that lasted long.) Mary Baker has a theory that these fights were like the mating

At the Ralph Warrens' apartment, in New York. The only thing the picture proves beyond a doubt is that Mayo didn't wear garters. Mr. Warren, the photographer, remembers the incident but none of the details, which is probably just as well.

dance of the whooping crane, as a sort of prelude to love, but again there are obvious exceptions. Like the Thanksgiving when the Raymond Masseys were having dinner with them, and as Mayo appeared with the turkey Bogie made some now-forgotten remark, and she hurled the turkey, platter and all, at his head. He grinned, and wiped the debris from his face, and they picked everything off the floor, rearranged it on the platter, and ate a cheerful meal.

There are occasional signs that they even took pride in these fights, although the reason is obscure unless it was that they fitted into the gangster image that was then his stock in trade. And if not pride there was certainly no reticence about them, as witness the letter he wrote to the Eric Hatches, regretting an invitation to a coming-out party. Eric's daughter Eve, and Mr. and Mrs. Carl Timpson's daughter Brenda, were to be presented to society at the Rockaway Hunting Club, on Long Island, in September of 1941, and because the Bogarts had been nice to Eve that summer she put them on the list. Bogie's reply, written in pencil, follows:

Dear Mr. and Mrs. Hatch

We, Mr. and Mrs. Bogart, are so distressed, and please tell Mr. and Mrs. Timpson, because we really feel it's going to cost too much.

For instance, just a glance at our estimated expenses should convince you that this matter is out of the question.

> Railroad fare $600
> Side trip to Grand Canyon (no sales resistance) $150
> 4 Indian Blankets $20 (no sales resistance)
> Hotel food in N.Y. (couple of hundred)
> Liquor on trip and in Twenty One (God knows!)
> Breakage (couple of hundred)

So as you can see this trip is really out of the question — please explain to the Timpsons.

Incidentally how well do you know the Timpsons — are you sure they aren't using you to further their own ends. I simply want to ask you one question — why should Miss Timpson come out before Miss Hatch — after all H comes before T in the alphabet, if we're going to be fair and democratic about all this.

Oh, and one more question — What are they coming out of — because I gather this is a mild "coming out party." And dear Mr. and Mrs. Hatch we haven't been to a tea dance since the Plaza Grill — cinnamon toast and martinis — never!!

And finally I've looked all thru Emily Post, Tiffany and an old book on behavior and convention and I can't figure out that Hewlett on the bottom to the left under R.S.V.P.

Is this Hewlett a place or the forgotten man who started the whole thing.

Anyway Mr. and Mrs. Bogart refuse with pleasure your kind invitation on account of how it's too far away — and anyway how do Mr. and Mrs. Timpson know our company would be pleasant.

You see, the whole thing's silly.

Love

Mayo and Bogie

As the then Mrs. Hatch remembers it, the "Breakage" item referred to a recent fight they'd had at the Algonquin, when they smashed an impressive amount of crockery and glassware. It was not for nothing that he nicknamed Mayo "Sluggy," a name which, in the true spirit of a yachtsman, he also gave his first boat. The Bogarts' neighbors on Horn Avenue remember night after night made hideous by the shouting and breakage, with an occasional and spectacular appearance of the combatants — as in the time they emerged from the house, Mayo leading him with a rope around his neck, while he shouted, "I'm going to hang you!"

The list of these encounters is all but endless, and only two more, for their own reasons, are worth recording. In 1943 they went to North Africa to entertain the troops (at one point in which trip she chased him over the

Lieutenant Bruce Cabot, Mayo, and Bogie in Casablanca during the Bogarts' 1943 trip to North Africa and Italy. The street urchin at the left is understandably dumbfounded.

rooftops of Algiers with a pistol), and on their return to New York they went to the Gotham, where Warner celebrities were usually stabled. Sam Jaffe, who with Mary Baker was Bogart's agent, recalls that his aunt-in-law, the mother of playwright Leonard Gershe, was in town, and she asked him if he thought Bogart would sign an autograph for her son (who at that point was admiring actors rather than writing for them). Jaffe said of course, and directed her to the Gotham, where it turned out that the Bogarts, still in battle dress from Africa, were in the middle of a full-fledged battle of their own, throwing lamps, furniture, and glassware at each other. Mrs. Gershe waited on the fringes, her autograph book at the ready, but before she could get in a word Bogart stamped out of the room and vanished. All through that night Mayo kept tearfully calling Jaffe, saying she'd driven Bogie away and now he'd probably been killed in traffic, and all through the night Jaffe had to listen to her muddled self-recriminations. Nobody heard from Bogie until the middle of the following morning, when he called Jaffe to check in.

"Where have you been?" Jaffe asked. "Mayo's been going out of her mind."

"I stayed with Helen," Bogie replied, referring to Helen Menken. It would appear that, as he hoped in his letter to Lyman Brown, they had remained friends. Mrs. Gershe, incidentally, never got the autograph.

Another, more serious fight had unexpected consequences. Bogart called the Jaffe-Baker office one day and said, "I think you'd better get over here; she's stabbed me." The partners rushed up to the Horn Avenue house, and there found Mayo hysterically insisting she hadn't done anything, in spite of the evidence of a long slash through the back of Bogart's jacket, through which blood was seeping. The knife lay on the kitchen table. They called Dr. Stanley Immerman, his doctor, who dressed the wound that was fortunately superficial, and it was then that Bogart asked his agents to take out an insurance policy on his life, and make themselves the beneficiaries. They demurred, but he pointed out that they'd invested a great deal of time and money in his career, and stood to lose it all if Mayo's aim should ever improve.

"Look at that seltzer bottle, there," he said, indicating a siphon bottle in the corner. "She threw it at my head and missed, but someday she might not miss, and I think you ought to have insurance. This is a thing where you never know what she's going to do."

So they took out a hundred-thousand-dollar policy on his life, and it remained in effect until long after he and Mayo were divorced. Then one day he came into the office, looking tan and fit after a weekend on his boat, and Jaffe said, "My God, you're going to outlive us all," and canceled the policy.

It could not in fairness be said that Mayo was the cause of his drinking, but during the time he was married to her he drank more than ever before or since — either to keep up with her, or because of the generally disorganized condition of the household. Also, the tenor of the time when Bogart first came to Hollywood was such that if a person went out on the town and *didn't* get drunk he was considered, in Allen Rivkin's words, "some sort of a fairy." It was a sign of masculinity to get drunk — the sign of a free man, who did as he pleased — and it also fitted the tough-guy image that was his trademark. It is no medical secret that in most people drinking brings on a change in personality, a releasing of hidden inhibitions, fears, or resentments, and Bogart was no exception. He could be enchanting when sober, and savage when drunk, and since he didn't show drunkenness in the usual manner the only way to tell if he was sober was by what he was doing. He didn't slur his words or stumble, but he did things that brought on acute remorse the next day. The sober Bogart bled for what the nonsober Bogart had done.

But this didn't keep him from drinking again, because that was what he liked to do. And the one rule he clung to above all others was that he lived his life as he wanted, with nobody to tell him what to do. That trait had first become evident in Andover, and it grew stronger with the passage of time. The only exception he ever made was to play parts that he didn't like, and even then he was adhering to another cardinal rule, which was to keep working. He fought against the bad parts but he took them, and as he gradually achieved top rank among the stars it followed that he had more to say about what he played.

He had been quiet and withdrawn when he was at Andover, and if it hadn't been for his status as a celebrity he would probably have remained that way all his life. He was not gregarious; he had a few close friends, some of whom seemed highly unlikely (Clifton Webb, for instance, whom he had known since his early days on Broadway and whom he referred to as Webby), and he had no compulsion to widen his circle. As a group he admired writers, although they were not exempt from the needling to which he submitted almost everyone on first meeting, to see if the relationship would be worth developing further.

But no celebrity is allowed total privacy, and the actor hasn't been born who doesn't, every now and then, like to hear a little cheering from the public. Acting is a precarious business, and actors, unless wholly carried away by their own ego, are insecure sometimes to the point of paranoia. Nothing bolsters a person's flagging confidence more than a bit of public adulation, and even those who have no need for it cannot try to deny that they don't like it. They can, of course, eventually become bored by it, but the honest ones will admit they'd be much more bored if it wasn't there. The sound of one hand clapping is no quieter than an actor whom nobody recognizes.

Thus Bogart grew to have two lives, his public life and his private life, and the diversity between the two and the apparent ease with which he coordinated them was remarkable. His first public image, of course (leaving aside the pretty-boy image of the early years), was Duke Mantee, the snarling, cold-eyed killer, and his life with Mayo fitted that pattern to perfection. Here the public and the private lives were nearly indistinguishable, but later on, when he remarried and settled down to raise a family, there came a drastic change. Gentle and sentimental, devoted to his wife and children, he was the antithesis of everything he'd been before, and the reconciling of the two sides was like the clashing of gears. One way he accomplished it was to retain the same front as before, and to take the hard-bitten approach to practically everything. On the surface he was the same person, using profanity almost like a trowel spreading mortar, and only occasionally, in unguarded moments, did the other side of him show through.

He would probably have denied this hotly, because he made it a fetish never to dissemble and always to be himself, but there were two totally opposite sides to his nature, and only one of them could be in command at a time. And it is a fair guess that the struggle between the two caused a certain amount of inner tension. Those who knew him best saw through the front — or sometimes didn't even see it at all — but his acting ability was such that he could convince almost everyone else. Playing this kind of part, day in and day out over a number of years, can take its toll on even the best actor. The The only time he could *really* relax was on his boat.

The best example of this diversity happened once when Philippe Halsman, the photographer, saw him getting off his boat in Newport Harbor. Halsman asked if he'd mind if he took his picture, and Bogart said of course not and added, "What do you want — Duke Mantee, Sam Spade, Rick — which one?"

"I just want you," Halsman replied. "Be yourself."

Halsman reported that Bogart's face went blank. (That is not to imply that the real Bogart was a blank; he simply didn't know which of his faces to wear.)

In many ways, he was a very private person. Few people outside his family can remember his saying anything particularly revealing about himself or his thoughts; most of his conversation had to do with the matter at hand at the moment, and only on rare occasions would he do any what might loosely be called philosophizing. His publicly expressed philosophy was simple: he believed that a man was either a professional or he was a bum; he believed that all phonies should be exposed; and he believed in saying what he felt like saying whenever and wherever he wanted. Those fairly basic thoughts were what the world was exposed to, and a slight hint of his more private side may be gleaned from the fact that he asked to have the Ten Commandments read at his funeral. He didn't obey them all to the letter, but he admired the spirit behind them. (The people with an unbroken record of adherence to the Decalogue could be tucked away and lost in one corner of Rhode Island.) He was religious without being a churchgoer; he was a Puritan who could use mule-skinner's language; he was a faithful husband who was married four times; and he was a sentimentalist whom some people considered a sadist. With that number of ingredients to his nature, it's a wonder he wasn't a raging schizophrenic. But in his own mind he was consistent, and that was all that mattered.

A number of budding careers have withered and died because of drink, and Bogart's might have suffered the same way if it weren't for the fact that he never let the drinking interfere with his work. No matter what he'd been doing the day before he was always on the set, in makeup and with his lines learned, at the appointed time, and his concentration was such that he could fight off the twitches and sweats of a hangover and still deliver an impeccable performance. He believed that the only thing he owed the public was a good performance, and no matter what else got in the way he would deliver it. To that end, in later years, he was in bed at ten o'clock on working nights, in order to get eight hours' sleep and be on the set and ready for shooting at nine o'clock sharp. He used to rebuke Sinatra for carousing the night away as well as taking his acting casually; he felt that that such an attitude was not professional.

Sam Jaffe has a theory that there are certain people who, if not actually mystics, are at least ordained for success or failure through something beyond their own power. He cites as a case in point the picture *High Sierra,* which was released in 1941 and which had been turned down by George Raft and Paul Muni for reasons of their own, and which Bogart took on his theory that an actor should always be acting. The script was by John Huston and W. R. Burnett, based on a novel of Burnett's, and it was directed by Raoul Walsh and had Ida Lupino as the female star. Bogart got the part by double default, and it was the beginning of a change in his career. He was still a gangster — a killer who's escaped from prison and is planning a holdup — but he was a different kind of gangster in that there was a softer side to him, a gentility and humanity that, oddly enough, corresponded with the gentler side of Bogart himself. Other pictures, such as *Angels with Dirty Faces* and *It All Came True,* had tried to soften the Duke Mantee image, but

As John Murrell in *Virginia City*. It's easy to see why he didn't often wear a moustache.

As the pseudo priest
in *The Left Hand of God*.

As Ray Earle in *High Sierra*.

As George Halley in
The Roaring Twenties.

As Marshall Quesne
in *The Return of Dr. X.*

An early publicity still,
possibly from the
white-thigh-and-tails days.

the scripts were transparent and the attempts unconvincing. In *High Sierra*, thanks partly to the script and partly to Bogart's sensitive interpretation, the audience was all on his side at the end, and when he was shot off the top of a mountain there was sympathy for him instead of the satisfaction that usually accompanied his demise. He had been second-billed below Ida Lupino in this picture, but in the next and all subsequent ones he received top star billing.

The next one was a strange picture, a bastard in more ways than one. Four years previously he had been in *Kid Galahad* (third-billed beneath Edward G. Robinson and Bette Davis), a prizefight story based on the novel by Francis Wallace. It had enjoyed a respectable success, so now Warner Brothers, working on the theory that what was good once would be just as good a second time, took the same novel and made it into a circus story, calling it *The Wagons Roll at Night*. (By odd coincidence, the picture Bogart did immediately preceding *High Sierra* was titled *They Drive by Night*.) The framework of *Wagons* was identical to *Galahad*, with a mad lion substituted for the prizefighter, and Sylvia Sidney for Bette Davis. Bogart gave the picture exactly what it deserved: a competent performance, and no more. He later referred to it, if at all, as "that picture I did after *High Sierra*."

He had got *High Sierra* by double default, and now, by single default, he got what some people still consider the most brilliant picture he ever did. It was *The Maltese Falcon*, written and directed by John Huston from the novel by Dashiell Hammett, and Raft turned it down on the ground that Huston was an unknown director and nobody with whom he should risk his reputation. So Bogart played Sam Spade, the private eye, and the gangster image was gone for good. A new image was born, and it can best be described by what *The New Yorker*, thirty-two years later, wrote about one of the picture's periodic revivals:

> The star is Humphrey Bogart, in his most exciting role, as Sam Spade, the private detective who is an ambiguous mixture of avarice and honor, sexuality and fear. This brilliant first film directed by John Huston is hard, precise, and economical — an almost perfect visual equivalent of the

Life with Mayo wasn't *all* fighting, as these pictures, taken by Eric Hatch, demonstrate.

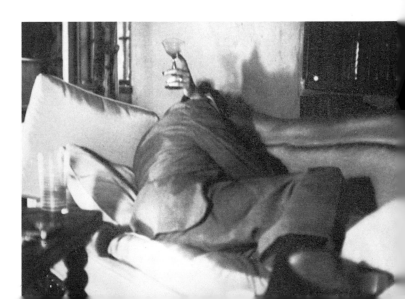

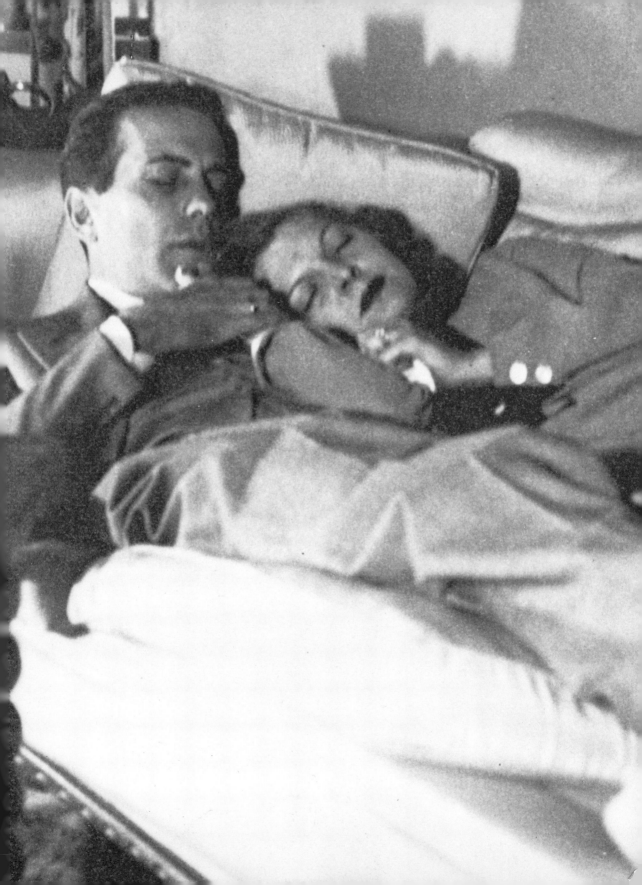

Dashiell Hammett thriller. Bogart is backed by an impeccably "right" cast: Sydney Greenstreet, Mary Astor, Peter Lorre, and Elisha Cook, Jr., as Wilmer.

And there is the basis for Jaffe's theory: Bogart had literally backed into the two parts that got his career off dead center, and had it not been for them he might have gone on playing gangster roles until he was too old to be convincing. It could be argued that sooner or later the right part would have been bound to come along, but the filling stations and haberdasheries are bristling with talented actors for whom the right part never appeared. And, as a side thought on fate, Jaffe likes to ponder what *The Maltese Falcon* would have been like if Raft had taken the part; would it have been the same picture? There will be a three-second pause for pondering.

Mayo's passionate desire to see him stop playing heavies was now apparently realized, and in only one of his next three pictures did he die in the end. This was a mishmash called *The Big Shot*, which had him as a three-time loser trying unsuccessfully to go straight, and it combined echoes of *High Sierra* with some of the more shopworn gangland clichés. His credo that he owed the public a good performance was put to a severe test by this and by occasional pictures like it; there was no challenge, and nothing to do but hope it would soon be over.

The advent of World War II to the United States put an effective end to all gangster pictures, because there was now a set of heavies that made gangsters look like Mrs. Wiggs of the Cabbage Patch. As a broad generality, it can be said that pictures that are long on patriotism are short on artistic merit, but every now and then one crops up that has just the right mixture of both, and the effect can be electric. After *The Big Shot*, Bogart made a war/espionage picture, *Across the Pacific*, which had the advantage of being directed by John Huston (although he left for war service before it was completed), and while it was well received at the time it has become lost in the pyrotechnics and clouds of nostalgic smoke surrounding the next one, a war/melodrama/romance called *Casablanca*. This picture was the ultimate proof of Jaffe's theory in that all its elements — timing, cast, and story — jelled

Across the Pacific. He was no longer a heavy, but he still took a beating.

at an instant that could probably never be duplicated again, and they jelled in a way that would make a mystic give credit to some astral power rather than the mortals involved in its production. *Casablanca* was and remains a phenomenon, and it shot Bogart into an orbit in which he still floats, serene, above the lesser drudges who toil before the cameras.

But Mayo, whose ultimate hope had been to see him as a romantic lead, found hemlock in the heady wine of his success. If she had been jealous of any passing girl on the Newport docks, imagine the rages of her jealousy at seeing him play love scenes with Ingrid Bergman; she convinced herself he was in love with her (disregarding the fact that he would have only been joining half the male population of the world), and she behaved in a correspondingly unbridled way. When, after the picture had opened, someone complimented Bogart on his performance, he smiled thinly and said, "I wasn't allowed to see it."

Mayo, without realizing it, had climbed aboard her own petard, and was busily priming the fuse.

For the benefit of Sherpas, the newly born, and others who may not
have seen *Casablanca*, a brief summary of the story would seem to be in order.
Bogart played the part of Rick, a cynical American adventurer who owns
a nightclub in Casablanca, a way station for refugees trying to escape to the
New World from the Nazis. The time is early December 1941; Pearl Harbor
has not yet been attacked, and many Americans are still uncommitted.
Ilsa Lund (Miss Bergman) shows up at the nightclub with her husband Victor
Laszlo (Paul Henreid), a Resistance fighter who is fleeing the Nazis. At
the time of the fall of Paris she had a brief but intense affair with Rick; she
thought Laszlo dead at the time, and when she found he was alive she
vanished without explanation, leaving Rick understandably wounded and
bitter. Now it turns out that Rick has two exit visas, which will allow Ilsa and
Victor to escape, but the memory of the jilting is still fresh, and he is
tempted to withhold them. At a clandestine meeting Ilsa first tries to get them
by threatening him with a gun, then says she is still in love with him; she
says she left him once but could never do it again, and is now prepared to run
away with him. He pretends to agree, but in the end he gives the passes
to Ilsa and Victor, allowing them to escape.

The story was originally a play, *Everybody Goes to Rick's*, by Murray
Burnett and Joan Alison, and it died before it ever reached Broadway. But
Warners had already bought the screen rights, so to salvage what they could
they assigned Julius J. Epstein and his brother Philip to try to put some-

101

The famous scene from
Casablanca.

thing together. Hal B. Wallis, the producer, wanted Miss Bergman for the female lead, but she was under contract to David Selznick and could be loaned out only on the promise of a superior picture, so Wallis sent the Epsteins over to Selznick to ad-lib the property into something impressive. This they did, although basically all they had were a few scenes and ideas for a few more. Another screenwriter, Howard Koch, was assigned to help out, and then (this was shortly after Pearl Harbor) the Epsteins were given leave to go to Washington to work on the "Why We Fight" series, under the newly minted Major Frank Capra. This left Koch alone with the script for about four weeks, trying to put together something that looked like a story, and then the Epsteins returned and all three writers pitched in — not necessarily in total harmony. By the time shooting started, only half the screenplay was finished.

The actors had done their homework as best they could. Miss Bergman makes it a rule, if she doesn't know her leading man, to see his pictures before she meets him so she'll know what to expect, and in Bogart's case she saw *Maltese Falcon* over and over again. She was, if not nervous, at least apprehensive about meeting him because of his reputation; when they met, he was kind and gentle and considerate, and not at all what she'd expected. But he was also grumpy and upset, because of the condition of the script, and he spent most of his lunch hours wrangling with Wallis over what was going to happen to the story. (Those lunch hours he wasn't with Wallis he was likely to be hounded by Mayo, who was keeping a hawk eye on him and Miss Bergman and doing nothing whatsoever to improve people's dispositions.)

Bogart's preparation for the picture had been of another sort. Before shooting began, Mel Baker said to him, "This is the first time you've ever played the romantic lead against a major star. You stand still, and always make her come to you. Mike [Curtiz, the director] probably won't notice it, and if she complains you can tell her it's tacit in the script. You've got something she wants, so she has to come to you." Bogart absorbed the advice in silence, and he followed it in every scene except one. In the scene where she pulls the gun on him, he says, "All right, I'll make it easier for you. Go ahead and shoot. You'll be doing me a favor." Then the stage directions read *Rick*

104

walks toward Ilsa. As he reached her, her hand drops down. That was one
of the few exceptions.

Generally speaking, the shooting was a shambles. It was done on a day-to-day
basis, with Curtiz scanning the various scripts as they came hot from the
typewriters, and saying things like, "This looks interesting. Let's try this one
today." The actors, without the security of a finished script or even the
knowledge of where they were heading, became jittery and upset, and when
they asked Curtiz for guidance he'd simply say, "Actors! Actors! They
want to know everything!" It wasn't even known whether Miss Bergman would
end up with Bogart or Henreid, and when she told Curtiz she *had* to know,
in order to be able to play the scenes correctly, he replied, "We don't know.
Just play it day to day, and we'll see what happens." One day, when Bogart
appeared for shooting, Curtiz told him, "You've got an easy day today.
Go on that balcony, look down and to the right, and nod. Then you can go
home."

"What am I nodding at?" Bogart asked. "What's my attitude?"

"Don't ask so many questions!" Curtiz replied. "Get up there and nod,
and then go home!"

Bogart did as he was told, and didn't realize until long afterward that that
nod had triggered the famous "Marseillaise" scene, where Henreid leads the
nightclub orchestra in drowning out some Germans who'd been singing
"Die Wacht am Rhein." It's a scene that even after thirty years prickles the
scalp and closes the throat, and for all Bogart knew he was nodding at
a passing dog.

There was still the matter of the ending. The convolutions of the pilot are
such that it isn't until almost literally the last minute that Rick tells Ilsa
he isn't going with her, and with everything except that final moment shot and
in the can it was clear a decision had to be made. The decision was typical:
shoot two endings, and see which feels better. (Henreid, incidentally, had been
loud in his insistence that he get the girl; to him, there were no two ways

The other famous scene from *Casablanca*.

Two more *Casablanca* love scenes.

"When the camera moves in on that Bergman's face, and she's saying she loves you, it would make anybody look romantic."

about it.) So they wrote two endings; they shot the first, and that was it.
It was perfect because everyone had been wanting the other one, and yet
recognized that it couldn't happen. If Bogart had got the girl he would
have appeared somehow sleazy and underhanded; by giving her up he made
a noble gesture, aided the forces of good, and had a beautiful exit line,
as he walked off into the night with the chief of police. It was probably just as
well the actors didn't know where they were headed, because that made
the final twist all the more of a jolt for the audience. It was the head-versus-
heart dilemma, played out to the final scene.

In addition to the principals, there was a first-rate supporting cast. Claude
Rains played the corrupt Vichy chief of police, and the others included
Sydney Greenstreet and Peter Lorre (both of whom had been with Bogart in
Maltese Falcon), as well as Conrad Veidt, S. Z. Sakall, and Dooley Wilson,
the pianist who played the unforgettable "As Time Goes By." And this
would be as good a time as any to settle the matter of "Play it again, Sam."
In spite of the fact that Woody Allen wrote a play by that title, in which
he saw himself as the epitome of everything Bogartian, and in spite of the fact
that people swear they heard it in the picture, those exact words were never
spoken. When Ilsa requests the song she says, "Play it once, Sam, for old
time's sake," and when he demurs she says, "Play it, Sam. Play 'As Time
Goes By.' " Then, later, Rick says, "You played it for her and you can
play it for me," and when Sam is still unwilling he snarls, "If she can stand
it, I can. Play it!"

By now this straightening out of the record is undoubtedly too late, and "Play
it again, Sam," has joined "I knew him well, Horatio," in the lexicon of
misquotations.

On November 8, 1942, Allied forces landed on the coast of French North
Africa, specifically at Oran, Algiers, and Casablanca. It was as though
Warner Brothers had planned the invasion; eighteen days later, on Thanks-
giving Day, *Casablanca* opened at the Hollywood Theatre in New York.
As though that weren't enough, its general release came on January 23, 1943,
in the middle of the conference between Roosevelt and Churchill at Casa-

blanca. Because of wartime security the conference couldn't be publicized at the time, but its subsequent news stories did nothing whatsoever to harm the picture. If anything, they tended to point up the allegorical similarity between Rick and Roosevelt: the uncommitted American who stands by while others do the fighting, and then at the proper time steps in and turns the tide. A great deal of allegory has been read into *Casablanca* since its opening, much of it pure drivel, but the Rick-Roosevelt similarity is too strong not to merit passing mention.

The critics filled the air with flaming pinwheels of praise. The picture was nominated in eight categories of the Academy Awards and won in three: Best Picture, Best Screenplay, and Best Director. It brought Bogart his first nomination as Best Actor, but he lost out to Paul Lukas in Lillian Hellman's *Watch on the Rhine*. Although *Casablanca* has since, in cold retrospect, been called "the best bad picture ever made," there have been no second thoughts about Bogart; his image has grown to a point somewhere near idolatry, and shows no immediate sign of diminishing. His own reaction to his new status was typical.

"I didn't do anything I've never done before," he replied once, when the subject of his romantic qualities came up. "But when the camera moves in on that Bergman's face, and she's saying she loves you, it would make anybody look romantic." There is more truth to that remark than most actors would care to admit.

The British Broadcasting Corporation recently did an hour-long special on Bogart's life, and on the subject of him as a romantic they cited Jack Warner's skepticism. Warner is supposed to have said, before *Casablanca* was filmed, "Who the hell would ever want to kiss Bogart?" and Miss Bergman is supposed to have replied, "I would." It made the point nicely, and while Miss Bergman has issued no flat denials, her rejoinder is to smile and say she doesn't recall ever making such a statement. Her own statement is much more eloquent; when pressed for an interview about Bogart, she replied with a remark that could very easily be the title of a book: "I kissed him, but I never really knew him."

Alistair Cooke, one of those interviewed on the BBC program, was to a certain extent in agreement with Sam Jaffe as to the reason for Bogart's enormous success. He didn't cite any mysticism but he did stress timing, and if you want to look at it one way that can be the same thing. He pointed out that Bogart's timing was such that he was playing the bad guy when bad guys were all the rage, and then when Hitler and Mussolini took over the role of bad guys the hero had to be someone tough; the marcelled-hair crowd, as he called them, couldn't make it any more. And with this Miss Bergman is in complete agreement, backed up by testimony from her daughter Pia. The young these days don't want their heroes pretty, she says — Nelson Eddy or Robert Taylor or Rudolph Valentino wouldn't be worth cold snail tracks — and she cites Pia's fascination with the bullfighter Belmondo. "How can you like him?" she once asked her daughter. "He's an animal." Pia's reply was direct and to the point: "What's the matter with that?" And there, she believes, is one of the many indirect reasons for the longevity of *Casablanca*.

The immediate, and direct, effect of the picture was to get Bogart a goodly package of money, make him top dog on the Warner lot, and drive Mayo closer to the rim of insanity. She, who had thrown crockery at Tay Garnett to get a romantic part for her husband, now saw him become world famous as his own type of romantic hero — the cynic who's been wounded in love but has not lost his gallantry — and his romantic partner was one of the loveliest dishes ever to grace the screen. He must be in love with her — he'd be crazy not to be — and the more Mayo brooded about it the more desperate she became. And if the normal Mayo was a bad drunk, the desperate Mayo made Attila the Hun look, in comparison, like an Irish tenor.

To be fair to Mayo, she was wildly in love with him; her main problem was control. It was in December of 1943, more than a year after the invasion, that they went to North Africa, but she somehow had the picture of Bogie wading ashore in the teeth of German machine-gun fire. With friends at "21" before they left, she became maudlin about how, if he was going to die, she wanted to die with him, and while her exact conversation has faded into the mists of time, phrases like "I love that son of a bitch so much," and "If they're going to get him they're going to get me," come drifting back. The party then progressed to Jack Bleeck's Artist & Writers Restaurant, where, if memory serves, she came under the impression that everyone in the bar was German. Bogie simply sat back and laughed.

They were abroad for three months, entertaining the troops in camps, hospitals, and field units in North Africa and then in Italy. The exact script of their act is unrecorded, but the Bogart presence was all that was needed. Their visit to Italy was truncated one night, when what turned out to be a high-ranking general called to complain about the noise coming from their hotel room. Bogart told the caller exactly where he could stuff his complaint, and the next morning they were removed from that theater of operations. Film clips of their trip (minus the encounter with the general), plus shots of combat with Bogart's voice-over narration, were put together into a short for the Red Cross entitled *Report from the Front*. It was distributed free to participating theaters for what was called Motion Picture Theatres Red

114

Overleaf: An extraordinary shot, by Gjon Mili, of the sound stage for *Action in the North Atlantic.* Bogart and Massey are at right center, while the grips and technicians go about their various jobs. In the left background, a man walks down the studio street in the Burbank sunlight.

Cross Week. Another war-effort picture, if such it could be called, was *Thank Your Lucky Stars,* a pastiche of what later became known as cameo performances by Bogart, Eddie Cantor, Bette Davis, Olivia de Havilland, Errol Flynn, John Garfield, etc., etc. Neither the picture nor anyone in it was nominated for an Academy Award.

The first real picture he did after *Casablanca* was *Action in the North Atlantic,* a film that had started out as a short tribute to the Merchant Marine and was expanded into a full-length feature. As its title implies, it dealt with the rigors of convoy duty, and it was chockablock with all the time-tested bromides about men at war. It was, however, an exciting picture, thanks mostly to the special-effects department, which put together convincing tank shots of convoys, as well as fires and explosions and general carnage wild enough to trigger the adrenalin in the most blasé picturegoer. The double-spread picture in this book shows the lengths to which they went: a whole section of a merchant ship has been built on the sound stage, and the smoke and flames of battle are governed by a man at a console who, almost as though he were playing an organ, touches the various switches in a preprogrammed pattern that makes the explosions seem random but still manages to miss the actors. Raymond Massey, who played the captain, and Bogart, his exec, can be seen about dead center, dwarfed by all the special effects around them.

One day when they had, as they thought, completed the abandon-ship scene and were through work for the day, Bogart and Massey went to a bar near the studio and began to make plans for what they'd do with the afternoon that was left to them. They ordered two double martinis and thought it might be nice to shoot some golf; after two more doubles they decided

115

The abandon-ship scene in *Action in the North Atlantic*. Bogart and **Massey** are
brimful with martinis, and J. M. Kerrigan, seated beneath them, has just said,
"Do you think all this realism is going to affect the legitimate theater?"

golf was out of the question, so they ordered another round, this time singles. They were toying with other recreational possibilities, and were about to order a further round of martinis when a man from the sound stage put his head in the door and said they had to redo the abandon-ship scene.

"The hell with it," Bogie replied. "Let the doubles do it."

"We need your voices," the man said. "Everybody's waiting."

"My double is braver than your double," Massey announced, as though it mattered.

"He is like hell," said Bogie. "My double is the bravest double there is."

"Gentlemen," said the man from the sound stage. "Everyone is —"

Nobody listened to him, as the two actors fell to wrangling over whose double was the braver, and then the argument developed into which of *them* was the braver, and before they really intended it they were back on the sound stage, ready to abandon ship all over again. Also in the lifeboat with them was J. M. Kerrigan, an old-time character actor whose roots went back into the silent pictures and the theater. The flares and the smoke pots were lighted, the cameras started to roll, and slowly the lifeboat slid down the side of the ship. The man on the console did his work well, although Bogart had the seat of his pants slightly singed, and as they gasped their way through the smoke and flame Kerrigan said, in his heavy brogue, "Do you think all this realism is going to affect the legitimate theater?" Luckily, there was enough other noise so that the boom mike didn't pick up his voice. Neither Bogart nor Massey could have gone through the scene again that day.

The making of a motion picture is a long, tedious business, and anything that can relieve the monotony is welcome. For every shot the public sees there have been anywhere from one to fifty retakes; every new setup must be lighted and tested to everyone's satisfaction, and when the special-effects crew is turned loose whole hours may pass while they put together some par-

119

The Treasure of the Sierra Madre.
A far cry from the "sprig
of aristocracy" in *Swifty.*

This is how he looked
in *To Have and Have Not,*
his first picture with Betty.

Passage to Marseilles.
This is how he looked
when he first met Betty.

As Fred C. Dobbs, in *The Treasure of the Sierra Madre.*

The beginning of Queeg's breakup in *The Caine Mutiny.*

ticular bit of business. In the circumstances it is hardly surprising that some people turn to harmless practical jokes to pass the time, and Bogart was always on the lookout for such a diversion. In the cast of this picture was a young actor whose real name was deemed unsuitable for the billboards, but for whom no screen name had yet been found. Jack Warner was supposed to be working on it, but as yet had come up with nothing. One day an imp prodded Bogart into action. He took the young actor aside, and said, "Warner's finally got a name for you. It's great."

"What is it?" the man asked.

"José O'Toole."

"*What?*" The man was flabbergasted.

"José O'Toole. It's got all the right ethnic implications, and besides there's a sort of lilt to it. Warner's very hot on it."

The man went storming off to Warner's office in a rage, and was well into his tirade before Warner was able to get a word in and convince him of his innocence. Massey, who'd been in on the plot, chortled with Bogart over the incident the rest of the day.

⌗

His last picture of 1943 was, predictably, another war story. For the first time since *Stand-In* Warners loaned him out, this time to Columbia, for a picture called *Sahara*. The story was a reasonably straightforward one, about a tank crew in the Libyan Desert, but the writing credits were so insanely complicated as to warrant reproduction here. They follow: "Screenplay by John Howard Lawson and Zoltan Korda. Adaptation by James O'Hanlon. From an original story by Philip MacDonald, based on an incident in the Soviet film *The Thirteen*." All that was needed was an "additional dialogue" credit to complete the bouillabaisse. As war stories go it was a good

Young Miss Bacall, age nine, at Highland Manor girls' school,
in Tarrytown, New York.

At St. Augustine. The French sailors are either blind or stuffed; otherwise they would not have their backs turned.

At St. Augustine, when she drove the Seabees mad with desire.

Betty's first *Harper's Bazaar* cover, during World War II.

Considering the period,
this was cheesecake
of the most provocative sort.

Another cheesecake shot,
in which she looks
all of eleven years old.

one, and Bogart was properly tough and determined as the tank commander.
He was what people liked to think of as the typical American soldier; if
the typical American soldier *had* been like him, the war would have been won
two weeks after we landed.

He made just one picture in 1944 — not counting *Report from the Front* —
and this was *Passage to Marseille*, back at Warners with the old *Casablanca*
combination of Wallis, Curtiz, Rains, Greenstreet, and Lorre. But there
the similarity ended; Bogart played a French journalist who escapes from
Devil's Island, where he was sent after being framed by the government,
and joins the Free French and is subsequently killed on a bombing mission.
It was an elaborately constructed picture, with flashbacks within flashbacks,
but the confusion was mitigated by solid performances from all hands.

It was during the making of this picture that Howard Hawks dropped by
the set, bringing with him a young lady he had recently taken under contract.
She was nineteen years old; a graduate of the Julia Richman High School,
in New York, she had studied at the American Academy of Dramatic Art,
and had started her theatrical career as an usher at the St. James Theatre.
Before being discovered by Hawks she had been one of the hotter fashion
models for *Harper's Bazaar;* when, during the war, she went to St. Augustine,
Florida, with Diana Vreeland, then fashion editor of the *Bazaar,* to model
some sports clothes, the resident Seabees were so stunned at the sight of her
that they wrote to the magazine by the hundreds, asking her name. It
rained a good deal during that trip, and she would sit in the hotel room with
Mrs. Vreeland, spinning out her dreams and her determination to become an
actress ("Do you think Rita Hayworth is a good dancer? I can dance better
than she can," and so forth). She used to stand outside Sardi's, in New
York, watching the celebrities come and go and in this way feeling a little
closer to the theater. She was born Betty Perske, in Brooklyn, but when
her father vanished into the woodwork her mother resumed her maiden name
of Bacall. A press agent had thought up the name Lauren as being more
slinky than Betty, and she loathed it. She was tall, svelte, and beautiful (an
element of Russian in her ancestry was responsible for her sleek, tawny
hair, and wide-apart eyes that seemed always to be looking at you from a

In this scene from
To Have and Have Not,
his interest is in more than
just lighting her cigarette.

With Betty in *The Big Sleep*.

The bride and groom at Malabar Farm on May 21, 1945.

pillow), and when Hawks introduced her to Bogart she towered over him by a matter of inches. It was a how-do-you-do meeting, and that was all, although she now thinks that Hawks was probably, so to speak, testing the water.

The following year, Warners decided to take Ernest Hemingway's novel *To Have and Have Not* and see if they could make it into another *Casablanca*. Hawks was the producer-director, the screenplay was by Jules Furthman and William Faulkner, and Bogart, naturally, was the star. Instead of Miss Bergman they had Miss Bacall, and instead of Dooley Wilson at the piano they had Hoagy Carmichael, and the story concerned Bogart's conversion from strict neutrality to being an active abettor of the Free French. The first words he spoke to his leading lady, after their meeting the previous year, were, "I saw your test," and then he delivered himself of one of the thundering understatements of the century: "We'll have a lot of fun together."

Hawks later said it was lucky for the picture they fell in love, because the electric current that crackled between them made it considerably easier on the director. At that point Betty's acting skills were more latent than evident, but her feeling for Bogie — and his for her — needed no assists from behind the camera. She was twenty years old but she looked ageless; she was the eternal temptress, with the sideways glance and the silken, throaty voice. Her first line on screen: "Does anyone here have a match?" set the tone for the performance, and when she sang "How Little We Know" it was clear that a new personality had arrived. She joined the ranks of the "The" actresses, for whom the press agents turned common nouns into proper ones: Clara Bow, the "It" girl; Ann Sheridan, the "Oomph" girl; Marie MacDonald, "The Body"; and now Lauren Bacall, "The Look." Mercifully her talent overcame her epithet, which was soon forgotten.

The picture when completed bore little or no relation to Hemingway's book, but that was of secondary importance to its romantic interest. Betty's most-quoted line came as she undulated out of Bogart's hotel room; she gave him the sideways look over her shoulder, and said, "If you want me, just whistle. You know how to whistle, don't you, Steve? You just put your lips together, and — blow." That line became another "Play it, Sam," except for some reason people were able to remember it correctly. Its importance to the two characters involved can be gauged from the fact that he gave her a small, gold whistle as a memento.

Mayo had fought off all the phantom competition like a tigress; now that the real thing had arrived it was almost as though she sensed the futility of trying to fight any longer. She didn't give up immediately — far from it — and she wasn't fooled when Sam Jaffe or Mary Baker told her Bogie was out with "the cast," but she was fighting a rear-guard action and she knew it. On May 10, 1945, she and Bogie were divorced, and he and Betty were married eleven days later, on Louis Bromfield's Malabar Farm, in Ohio. He was aware of the twenty-five-year difference in their ages, but if it caused him any hesitation it didn't show; it was as though he sensed this was the marriage he'd been looking for all along.

Their age difference was emphasized by the fact that, early in their romance, he called her "Baby," a name that was picked up by the press and continued for some little while. Shortly after the marriage Bogie ran into Ester Leeming, his friend from *Petrified Forest* days, as he was leaving "21," and he gave her his usual greeting: "Hiya, Pepita." (She had played Paula, the Mexican cook.)

"I hear you married Lauren Bacall," she said, stating the case mildly; the courtship and marriage had used up almost as much newsprint as the Spanish-American War.

"Yeah," he replied, with a smile. "Baby's a real Joe."

What he meant was obvious, but the words taken out of context could have meant almost anything. It was a relief to everyone when the "Baby" nickname faded from public use and was replaced by her given name. Nowadays, anyone who calls her "Lauren" or "Baby" is on the market for a thick lip.

A sidenote on her character: She is and always has been a lady of iron determination, unshakable loyalty to whatever or whoever she may be involved with, and a no-nonsense approach to getting things done. Back in the days when she was an usher at the St. James Theatre, the critics Richard Watts, Jr. and George Jean Nathan and the writer William Saroyan were attending a repertory performance of Gilbert and Sullivan, and they tarried on the sidewalk between acts after all the other playgoers had gone in. Betty came out and shooed them in like so many tardy schoolboys, saying words to the effect of "All right, you three, get it inside," and they were so enchanted that Nathan and Saroyan decided to become better acquainted with her. Much later, when she was a celebrity, Nathan sent Watts a clipping about her, reminding him of where they had first met. Nobody was surprised that she had gone on to higher and greater things.

A NUMBER OF THINGS changed for Bogart during the 1945–1946 period, a sort of clearing of the air and turning over a new leaf and flexing the muscles he'd been developing over the past decade or so. He had a new bride, one who neither encouraged nor necessitated his drinking with both hands; he had a new boat, the fifty-four-foot yawl *Santana*, which replaced the in-more-ways-than-one obsolete *Sluggy*; and he had a new house, in Benedict Canyon, a step up from the battle-scarred Horn Avenue place. And, last but not least, he signed a contract with Warner Brothers that was and still must remain unique: it gave him one million dollars a year over a period of fifteen years, thereby guaranteeing him walking-around money until he was sixty-one and eligible for Social Security. Few actors have had such a platinum-studded future guaranteed them, but not many have worked so hard for it. He had, at the age of forty-six, been in eighteen plays and fifty-three pictures, a score that many an older actor would envy.

The house, at 2707 Benedict Canyon Road, was up a long driveway near the head of the canyon, hidden from public view and as rustic as one can get in Beverly Hills. It had a cozy, pub-type bar (he didn't give *up* drinking when he divorced Mayo; he just eased off a bit), and in short order it acquired a menagerie consisting of one large dog, fourteen chickens, and eight ducks. Anent the drinking: Tay Garnett, in his memoirs, tells of someone's asking Bogart if he'd ever been on the wagon, to which the reply was: "Just once — and it was the most miserable afternoon of my life." On another

138

occasion, after a long lunch at "21," he announced he was going back to the hotel and take a nap, and when Betty said, "Sissy," he looked at her coldly and replied, "You stay drink-for-drink with me someday, and see if *you* don't need a nap." He was by no means a teetotaler, but he had lost the insecurity and general aggravation of the Mayo period, and could drink for pleasure rather than escape.

And a footnote to Mayo: She went back to her mother in Oregon, from where she would every now and then put through a drunken call to Mary Baker, trying to get to talk to Bogie. For obvious reasons he never spoke to her, and finally one night she called and said she was dying, and wanted to have one last word with him. That call drew a blank like all the others, and the next day she was dead, of what was generally conceded to be acute alcoholism.

As for Bogart, the only cloud on his horizon was one that worried him a lot less than it did Jack Warner. For reasons of his own he started taking hormone shots; the doctor warned him they might cause him to lose his hair, and they did. For him, the answer was simple: he bought a hairpiece that covered the damage until the hair grew back (and the first new growth came in with a sort of piebald effect), but for Warner it was the hideous specter of his fifteen-million-dollar romantic property shedding his hair like a milkweed puff. But the rug did its job well, and Bogart's romantic allure was undiminished.

As an actor, he had not yet branched out into the disparate roles that marked the later part of his career (a phony priest, a gold prospector, a river rat, a psychotic Navy officer), but his technique was all there, waiting only the chance to prove itself. And his technique was, very simply, concentration. If that seems oversimplification it is; it remains, however, the word he used for the *sine qua non.* In 1955, when he was doing a television version of *The Petrified Forest,* he asked Natalie Schafer what she thought was the most important element in acting, and when she said, "Vitality," he replied, "You're wrong — it's concentration." Miss Schafer says that his power of concentration was such that he was unaware of anything else that was going on around him, and while there is one known exception it will stand up as a general rule. In the television show, incidentally, Betty played the Peggy Conklin/Bette Davis part, and Henry Fonda the Leslie Howard part; Bogie kept an eye on Betty all through the rehearsals, never suggesting anything either to her or to Delbert Mann, the director, but aware of everything she was doing. To make an insanely farfetched simile, he was like a mother trout whose eggs have hatched in the Niagara River, and who is shepherding her young upstream, away from the falls. As for his performance, he was the same Duke Mantee who had chilled the audiences at the Broadhurst Theatre; after twenty years, he still had the part down cold. And that is an aspect of technique he didn't mention: being able to play the same role time after time with no loss in force or credibility. For a stage actor this is essential; a screen actor can forget the whole scene the minute the director says, "Print."

An actor's appraisal of himself is not necessarily reliable, because the combination of insecurity and ego that assails most sensitive performers can lead them into unsound conclusions, but most of his contemporaries feel that Bogart was intelligent enough, and self-analytical enough, not to be deluded about his acting. He and Spencer Tracy had great mutual admiration for each other's work, often saying, in a joking way, "After me, he's the best," although one time Bogart said to Jaffe, "Gary Cooper is not a great actor, but Tracy is. I'm not a great actor, but when we, Coop and I, come on screen, people focus attention on us." That, Jaffe believes, is what makes a star; that and great intelligence, which Bogart had. As witness the star quality, Jaffe once went on the set of *The Harder They Fall*, Bogart's last picture, and they were shooting a scene that involved Bogart and one of the more energetic of the Method actors. Between takes, Bogart whispered to Jaffe: "Watch this guy; he thinks he's going to steal the scene from me." They started a new take, and the Method actor screamed and punched and gave a good imitation of Westphalian ham, but when the rushes were shown it was only Bogart that people were looking at. He had two rules for playing with Method actors: (1) Let them improvise to their hearts' content, and just wait for your cue, and (2) Don't ever play an eating scene with them, because they spit all over you. Other than that, he found them harmless.

Signing the fifteen-million-dollar, fifteen-year contract, in 1947. Witnesses,
in addition to Betty, are Morgan Maree, his business manager, and
Sam Jaffe and Mary Baker, his agents.

Beyond the above quote to Jaffe, it's hard to find evidence of what Bogart thought of himself or of acting because, as producer Collier Young has pointed out, Bogart was the most un-actorish person he knew. He was two different people: a dedicated actor when at work, and when not at work he was one of a number of other people, and there was no shoptalk. Then there were subdivisions among those divisions; some actors who worked with him loved him and some loathed him, and the same went for his nonacting periods. He went his way unconcerned, behaving precisely as he felt the occasion demanded.

One example of an actor who would die for him is Billy Roy, who played the cabin boy in *Passage to Marseilles*. There was a scene where Roy had to throw an orange, and James Wong Howe, the cameraman, complained he threw like a girl. Time and again he tried, and Curtiz, the director, kept shouting "Cut!" while the grips and the extras began to jeer and whistle and stamp. Finally Bogart stepped in, stopped the shooting, and took Roy off to a corner of the set and taught him how to throw. Shooting didn't resume until he had it perfected, and there wasn't a peep from the jeering gallery. Later in the picture Roy was required to die in Bogart's arms, which was perfectly all right with him.

Then there is William Holden, whose opinion is that Bogart was "an actor of consummate skill, with an ego to match." The first picture in which they appeared together was *Invisible Stripes*, in 1939, when Holden was twenty-one, and there was a scene in which Holden had to drive a motorcycle while Bogart sat in the sidecar. Before the shooting started, Holden over-heard Bogart say to Lloyd Bacon, the director, "I won't ride with that son of a bitch; he'll crack it up. Get my double to do it." As Holden points out, when you're twenty-one you take the words "son of a bitch" seriously (as you get older, you learn they can even be a term of affection), and further-more he prided himself on his ability to handle a motorcycle. He did a slow, simmering burn, and when Bogart's double got into the sidecar and the shooting started, Holden was so determined to give an exhibition of good driving that he zoomed off and piled the machine into a brick wall. This set the tone for what might best be called a cool relationship, with Bogart taking no pains to hide his low opinion of Holden's ability. They weren't in another picture together until *Sabrina,* in 1954, in which there was a scene where Bogart was on camera while Holden read lines from the side, holding the script and, as it happened, smoking a cigarette. Bogart kept blowing his lines, and when finally Billy Wilder, the director, asked him what was wrong, he replied, "It's that fucking Holden back there, waving cigarettes around and throwing paper in the air." There was dead silence, and then Holden said to Wilder, "Shall I kill him now, or wait until later?" Frantically, Wilder worked to restore calm, and Holden said, "Look, Mr. Bogart, when you come to work on this set you're an actor; when I come I have to clean out the dressing rooms first." He decided against mayhem, because hitting a man twenty years his senior would have lost him the sympathy of everyone on the set. When shooting was over for the day, Bogart asked him to his dressing room for a drink, and after pouring two Scotches said, "I guess I got a little upset out there," to which Holden replied, "Let's just drink our Scotch, and forget it."

For what it may be worth, Holden has a theory that if an actor can be impersonated then he's not an actor but a personality. It is mentioned here only because in 1943 John Forsythe, then a fledgling actor, had worked out what was considered by all who saw it a clever impersonation of Bogart. On the set of *Destination Tokyo,* which was being made at Warners, Forsythe entertained some of his coworkers with the impersonation, and Cary Grant, the star of the picture, said, "Very good. Wait a minute and I'll get Bogart, and let him see it." He went over to where *Action in the North Atlantic* was being shot, while Forsythe tried to think of ways of vanishing from the face of the earth. In a few minutes Grant appeared with a faintly interested Bogart, and prodded Forsythe into repeating the impersonation. When it was over, Bogart sucked a tooth.

"One of us stinks," he said, and walked away.

His work habits have been touched on briefly; his routine was as unvarying as circumstances would allow. He came to work with a lunchbox containing two sandwiches and a bottle of beer; he'd take these to his dressing room

143

or trailer, and when the lunch break came he would divide it evenly, a half hour for the sandwiches and beer, and a half hour for a nap. He could lie down for a nap and be asleep in a matter of seconds. There were exceptions to this routine, as in the making of *Casablanca*, when he spent his lunch hours hassling over the script, and in the making of *High Sierra*, when he was left on top of a mountain while the rest of the company broke for lunch, but in general he adhered to it as much as he possibly could.

Another routine, and one that was unvarying, was the ten o'clock retirement on working nights. One Sunday evening, during the making of *The Harder They Fall*, he left Betty in charge of a group of friends while he went upstairs to bed, and the party, such as it was, went on for another two hours. At midnight Betty ushered the friends out, and as she came out the front door to say goodnight she inadvertently let the door close behind her. It was locked, as were all the other doors and windows; it being Sunday the servants were off, and she had no choice but to wake her husband. She rang the bell, and waited, and there was no answer. She rang again, and again, but there was still no sign that anyone had heard. Among the departing friends was the agent Irving Paul Lazar, a man of extremely short stature (Bogart once described him as the only living man who cheated at croquet by following his ball through the wicket standing up), and someone suggested they toss him to the second story, where there was an open window. Before this idea could be put into effect the front door opened, and there stood Bogart in a red dressing gown, glowering under the overhead light. It turned out he had heard the bell the first time and had thought it was his alarm clock; he'd gone into the bathroom and started to shave when the bell rang again, and it had taken him some little time to realize what was going on. In the circumstances he could have been excused a little profanity, but all he said was, "Good night, all," and then he and Betty went quietly inside.

On the subject of *The Harder They Fall*, there were intimations during the making of that picture that his health wasn't all it might be. There was nothing specific but he looked older, and seemed to tire more easily, and while it remained in the rumor category at the time a lot of people remembered it later on. There was one scene that could easily have been filmed as a refutation of all such rumors; it could have been Bogart's idea, or the director's, or it could have been total accident, but whatever the reason it was an effective countermeasure. All it was was a scene where he had to climb a long flight of stairs, but instead of walking up them he ran up, nimbly and on his toes; the camera followed him without a break as he went into his lines. He not only wasn't panting, he didn't even seem to be breathing, and while this effect would have been easy to achieve by cutting, this was one continuous shot, with no time out for him to catch his breath. Younger men than he would have been gasping and staggering after such a mountain-goat performance.

Generally speaking he was a tractable actor, willing to do anything the director suggested provided it seemed to make sense. If, however, things appeared pointless he would protest, as he did during the making of *The Desperate Hours* when William Wyler asked for another in a long series of retakes. Without rancor but with faint irritation, Bogart said, "Listen, Willie, when you say let's do it again do you want me to do the same thing again as I did before? If not, will you show me what you want, because there's no point sitting here doing it again time after time." Wyler took him aside and spoke some soothing words and the shooting continued, but he'd made his point and, whatever it was that Wyler said to him, he seemed satisfied. And on the set of *The Caine Mutiny* Stanley Kramer, the producer, was buzzing around giving suggestions to director Edward Dmytryk until finally Bogart said, "Look — either direct it yourself or leave this guy alone. You're just making him nervous." In short, he was tractable until he thought something was being done wrong, and then he asserted himself.

Edith Oliver's remark that "Bogart has class — he was such a gent!" is not only a good summary of the person himself, but also what he believed in. The word *class*, when used in the sense that means style, sums up a good deal of what he found important. If there were lapses in individual instances the overall picture remains constant, and his sense of style showed through in most of what he did. A successful person has no need to proclaim his success; it emanates from him like a faint flicker of St. Elmo's fire, and the man with true class is the one who carries it easily and without bombast. He may be deadly serious about himself and his ambitions, but on the surface he remains casual and unconcerned. Bogart had this mixture of the serious and the casual, and if on the surface he sometimes seemed to be overdoing the latter approach it didn't alter the fact that he was in grim earnest. The famous "grace under pressure" definition of greatness would be, obviously, the epitome of class, and there have been few better examples of grace under pressure than that given by Bogart in the last year of his life. Here his self-image was put to a terrible test, and it held up throughout the whole ordeal. Long before he was sick someone asked him if he was going to pick out a prep school for Steve, and his reply was "Hell no — I'll be dead by then," and that closed the matter. It also illustrated the matter-of-fact way he chose to regard his own mortality. If you were alive you were alive, and if you weren't then the hell with it.

His professionalism, already referred to, was a part of his class, as was the way he chose to live his life. There is probably a large majority of people for whom such a life would not be becoming or even desirable, but it was the way he wanted to live, and there was nobody who could make him change it. If he believed it was right then that was what he was going to do, and this attitude, while occasionally producing some irritating side effects, had about it the sort of class the songwriter was after in "I Did It My Way." Not everybody can get away with it, but those few who can are the ones who did it with class. There are some people who will argue that Bogart was simply an exhibitionist who caused severe rectal pains to all around him, but this argument neglects the fact that he could, when he chose, be as quiet and thoughtful as a Talmudic scholar. If he acted up, there was usually a reason for it, and the reason could often be found in the company.

Hollywood parties have, over the years, achieved the reputation of being Neronian orgies staged by Cecil B. DeMille, and the civilians of Pasadena, Los Angeles, and Pacific Palisades speak with envy of the "wild Hollywood parties" they have often heard of but never attended. In actual fact the parties, while undeniably expensive (it cost money to board over the swimming pool to make a dance floor, and even more money to build, as one

146

hostess did, the swimming pool only in order to board it over), are peopled to a great extent by married couples, some of whom drink too much but few of whom come completely unbuttoned. There have been parties when the entire company wound up in the (uncovered) swimming pool, and parties where people have done things they wouldn't do in front of the cameras, but by and large the people are well behaved, and if there is anyone who gets completely out of touch with reality it is often as not a visitor from the East, who feels he can let down his hair and howl. (One such, for whom Bogart unaccountably felt responsible, became a walking basket case at a party at Romanoff's, and Bogart spent the evening shadowing him to see that he didn't get into serious trouble.) By their very nature these parties contain a cross section of the movie business, which means that there will be a certain number of big shots, a certain number of phonies, and a certain number of people who are either trying to make face with, or have been turned off by, one or the other of the first two groups. In the circumstances it is not always the best place for a person to speak his mind, but for Bogart it was a challenge to do just that. The phonies, of course, were the ones he took on first, but once he was warmed up he would think nothing of taking on a big shot or two, just to keep his hand in. The top brass in Hollywood is inclined to believe its sycophants, and to look on itself with muted awe, and there was nothing that delighted Bogart more than shooting down someone with an overdeveloped sense of self-awe. The long-range result of all this was that there were certain houses to which he was not asked a second time, which was perfectly splendid as far as he was concerned.

He had an innate honesty that made him question anything that seemed wrong, especially in matters concerning himself. When he was getting two hundred and fifty thousand dollars for a picture it gave him a momentary twinge of worry, and in the course of a conversation with Jaffe he said, "Don't you think my salary's too heavy?"

"Put it this way," Jaffe replied. "That's what Tracy's getting."

Bogart considered this, then said, "OK. If Tracy gets it, then I want it, too."

He had total confidence in anything Jaffe told him; he respected Jaffe's integrity, and for him integrity was the most important thing there was, almost to the point of being an obsession. Lunching once with Jaffe and Betty at Romanoff's, he said, "If Sam says a thing is so then it's so, and I don't have to worry about it. I trust Sam more than anyone else in the world."

"Does that include me?" Betty asked.

He looked at her. "I said I trust Sam more than anyone else in the world," he said.

It was left at that.

His trust in Jaffe was based on a number of reasons, not the least of them the fact that Jaffe was a religious man and a dedicated family man, two traits not necessarily typical of the community. Also, and more important, Jaffe would stand up to him and, if the occasion demanded, tell him off, something few agents would do to a client of Bogart's importance. Once, at Romanoff's, he'd been needling Jaffe about something now long forgotten; he dug the needle in deeper and deeper, and finally went too far.

"Listen," Jaffe cut in. "I don't have to take that from you; nobody's going to say anything of that kind to me, and if you're going to keep on that way you can get yourself a new agent. I'll give you back your contract, but I'm not going to take any of that from you."

Bogart stared at him in silence for a while, then said, "OK," and the matter was dropped.

Another time the subject of fighting came up and Jaffe, who'd done a certain amount in his youth, told Bogart that if he ever got in a fight he'd be murdered; that he, Jaffe, could cut him to pieces because he didn't know the first thing about it. This, too, he accepted, and it added to his admiration for his agent. In passing, it should be noted that he was not a *total* stranger to fighting; back when he was married to Mary Philips they went to Connecticut

148

for a weekend with Stuart and Pat Rose, and at a yacht-club dance Rose became involved in a fracas — something that apparently was not unusual with him. Bogart came wading in to help, while Mary stood by and screamed, "Humphrey! Humphrey! Don't get your face hurt!" He might not have been good at it, but he was there when he felt he was needed.

One more item from the Jaffes should wrap up the reasons for his trust. Bogart arrived at their house one day slightly the worse for wear, most probably after a long and Drambuie-sodden lunch at Romanoff's. For some reason he took offense at their modernistic paintings, and began to ponder aloud whether he should throw something at them, or slash them, or just how he should show his disapproval. They let him ramble on, but finally, when it looked as though he might actually do something, Mrs. Jaffe lost her patience. "Go on," she said. "Get out." Bogart looked at her, incredulous, and she went on, "I don't like the way you're behaving. Get out of the house." Slowly, and slightly mystified, he left, but he left without rancor and he didn't refer to the paintings again.

IN SHORT, he admired those who stood up to him. His needling was often a test to see how people would react, and his judgment of them was based on how they responded. When he first met Sinatra, at The Players restaurant on Sunset Strip, he said, "They tell me you have a voice that makes girls faint. Make me faint." Sinatra replied to the effect that his opening was still a week off and he couldn't sing before then, and the matter was dropped. They became close friends, with a relationship that cast Bogart in an almost paternal role. Sinatra is noted for behaving precisely as he pleases, but in Bogart's company he was on his good behavior and was his most charming — which is as charming as the law allows.

Sometimes the targets were worthy of Bogart's testing, and sometimes they weren't; a lot depended on how much he'd had to drink. As an example of pointless needling: he met, at a Sunday night party at the Jaffes', a writer and book reviewer named Ben Ray Redman. He brooded over the name for a while, then said, "You know the trouble with you? You're just another of these goddam three-name writers — Clarence Budington Kelland, Thyra Samter Winslow, Mary Roberts Rinehart —" carried away with himself, he spun on — "Walter Pritchard Eaton, Stephen Vincent Benét, Margaret Culkin Banning, Celia Caroline Cole, Harriet Beecher Stowe, Hannibal Hamlin Garland, Louisa May Alcott, Marjorie Kinnan Rawlings —" until finally the host stepped in and put a stop to the harangue. Redman, powerless to deny the sin of having three names, hadn't been able to say a word.

150

Occasionally he would say something intended simply to get a rise out of a person, the nature of the bait always being governed by the amount of Scotch and/or Drambuie he'd consumed. At a party at Nunnally Johnson's, he went up to John Steinbeck and said, "Hemingway tells me he doesn't think you're all that good a writer." Steinbeck, who worked on the theory that a man's threshold of insult is directly proportionate to his intelligence, simply grunted and turned away, leaving Bogart with nothing more to say. And, on a more savage level, he accosted Lucius Beebe at "21," when Beebe and two friends were standing at the bar. For Bogart it was the end of a long lunch, and he brought his Drambuie with him as he came to the bar.

"Excuse me," he said, to Beebe. "Are you a homosexual?"

Beebe looked at him coldly. "I don't see what possible difference that makes to you," he replied.

"We have a bet on at our table," Bogart said. "Are you, or aren't you?"

"Then, if you insist," said Beebe, "no."

All three men stared at Bogart in silence, and he turned to one of the others. "Are you?" he asked.

"Only on Wednesdays," the man replied.

"And you?" he said, to the third.

"I try not to be."

By now aware that he was out on a limb with no place to go, Bogart put one hand behind his head, said, "Well, *I* am," and danced away. The three men turned back to the bar.

After about five minutes, Beebe said, "I think that was a rather rude question our actor friend asked," and with that he finished his drink, paid the check, and left.

(Apropos the Drambuie, once when the Bogarts had gone to New York, a friend in Hollywood went into Romanoff's and asked John, the bartender, if they had yet returned. John glanced at the oversized Drambuie bottle on the back bar, quickly estimated its contents, and said, "No, sir. Mr. Bogart's not back yet.")

He once said that "the only reason to make a million dollars in this business is to be able to tell some fat producer to go to hell," and it was in the needling of the top moguls that he took his greatest delight. Jaffe once got a call from Jack Warner complaining that at a big party Bogart had called him a creep. "You've got to do something about him," Warner said. Jaffe protested that he couldn't be responsible for Bogart's actions off the lot, but the next time he talked to him he told him that "Jack's upset because you called him a creep."

"Well, isn't he?" Bogart replied.

"That's not the point," said Jaffe.

"A man's either a creep or he isn't," said Bogart, and he continued to call Warner a creep every time he saw him thereafter.

Another, lesser mogul got the Bogart treatment in what turned out to be his jugular vein — in fact, his main aorta. He was a producer who was kept on the payroll by contributions from his mother, and he prided himself not only on his *bon mots* but also on the people to whom he had said them. He was a combination self-quoter and name-dropper, and Bogart destroyed him by saying, "You know, you're a terrible bore." The man turned ashen and began to foam at the mouth, and when he later complained to Jaffe and Jaffe relayed the complaint to Bogart, the result was the same as in Warner's case.

"Is he a bore, or isn't he?" was all that Bogart said, and that ended the conversation.

152

Another of his antagonists was a rotund agent named Paul Small (of whom it was said that "Paul Small casts a small pall"), and his needling of this individual reached a point where Small, enraged as a woman whose honor has been questioned, slapped him in the face. Bystanders pulled Small away and took him to an adjoining room, where they tried to calm him by telling him soothing things and saying this was just Bogart's way of having a little joke, but the more they explained the madder Small became, until he finally tore himself clear, ran into the other room, and slapped Bogart a second time.

Usually, however, these skirmishes ended short of physical violence, which was as Bogart intended, and sometimes his dodges to avoid combat were elaborate. At a party (these episodes usually happened at parties) he goaded the writer Julian Claman into stepping outside, "where we'll settle this right here and now," and when they reached the lawn he put an arm around Claman's shoulder and said, "Let's put on ladies' hats, and go back and make 'em all laugh." Another time, when invited outside, he told his opponent to go out and he'd be right with him; instead, he went to the bar and started a conversation with someone else, and when, several minutes later, the first man came looking for him, Bogart raised his glass and said, "Hi, there! Come in, and have a drink!" Probably the closest he ever came to extermination was at his own poolside, when he ripped into his friend and neighbor Sid Luft over a fancied wrongdoing (he had given Luft some business advice, which Luft hadn't followed). Luft, a man with an explosive temper and fists like Virginia hams, finally started for him, but before he got within range Bogart put out a hand and said, "All right, maim me — kill me if you want — but remember, I'm your brain. I do your thinking for you." Incredibly, Luft subsided, but it would have been a gory mess if he hadn't.

Exactly why he took pleasure in this form of recreation is anybody's guess. His hatred of phonies has already been mentioned, and it's possible that when he'd been drinking everybody began to look like a phony, but that isn't the whole answer; the only thing that's certain is that he was more savage drunk than sober. This leads to the too-easy answer that there was a Jekyll-Hyde syndrome brought on by alcohol, but that also leaves a lot of questions unanswered. Some people will say they never saw him mean, and others will say they never saw him anything but; there are those who will swear that his language was immaculate, and those who remember the occasional barracks language around the house; and there are women who recoil at the mention of his name, and women who remember him with warmth and affection. Betty Comden, the playwright, found him, in her words, "gallant and tender, attentive and adorable." (He used to ply her with stingers, saying, "I like that foxy face," which happens to be a perfect description; she has the face of a very beautiful fox.) A final possible answer is that he basically loathed the insincerity, sycophancy, and cowardice in Hollywood, and liked to think of himself as a rebel in a pack of proctophiles. The real reason is probably a combination of all of the above, with an additional X factor thrown in for good measure.

A determined effort has been made to keep the first person singular out of this narrative, on the theory that it is as distracting as a big, winking eye at the window, but there seems no way to avoid it in the following, and I think revealing, episode:

When I was working in Hollywood in 1955 and 1956, my wife came out to visit for a couple of weeks before Christmas. She had never met Bogart — or, if she had, only in passing — and she was terrified of his reputation for needling newcomers.

"What will I do if he picks on me?" she said. "I can't handle that sort of thing."

"If he picks on you, you pick right back," I told her. "Tell him you don't take any crap from bald men — tell him to put on his wig, and then you'll talk."

"I couldn't," she said. "I'd die."

We didn't run into the Bogarts until one night, when we were leaving Romanoff's after dinner, we came across them with a group of friends at the bar. Bogie beckoned us to join, and when the introductions had been made he said, "All right. Everybody back to our house."

"I have to go back to the Chateau for a minute," I said, referring to the Chateau Marmont, where we were staying. "We'll join you later."

"You go where you want," he said. "Mrs. Benchley's coming with me."

Trembling, Marjorie got into his black Thunderbird with him, and as they drove the few miles to his house he told her how glad he was she'd come out, how good he knew it would be for me, and if there was ever anything she needed, or if she wanted any help or advice, she was to call on him immediately. He was, in short, all the adjectives Betty Comden had used plus a few more; in the following days he took her on the boat, he talked with her about life and bringing up children, and by the end of her stay in Hollywood she was more than a little in love with him.

The next time I saw him, after she'd gone back, I said, "I think I should report that my wife has a thing for you."

He was embarrassed. "Tell her I'm really a shit," he mumbled. "Tell her I was nice only because she's new out here."

THE FIRST PICTURE he and Betty made as a husband-and-wife team (not counting a spot appearance in a thing called *Two Guys from Milwaukee*) was *The Big Sleep*, from Raymond Chandler's private-eye novel. It was an extension of the character he'd developed in *The Maltese Falcon*, but the plot of this one is so insanely involved that a description of it is all but impossible. If the players in *Casablanca* were confused during the shooting of the picture, those in *The Big Sleep* were totally at sea, playing each scene as it came along and hoping for the best. Only Howard Hawks's direction, and dialogue by the trio of William Faulkner, Leigh Brackett, and Jules Furthman gave the actors anything solid with which to work. Bogart was his usual professional self, and Betty, still in the early stages of learning her trade, made up in appearance what she lacked in professional finesse.

As usual, the critics were divided. Bosley Crowther of the *New York Times* wrote that "so many cryptic things occur amid so much involved and devious plotting that the mind becomes utterly confused," and added that "through it all, Humphrey Bogart stalks his cold and laconic way." He tossed a parenthetical dart at the leading lady: "Miss Bacall is a dangerous looking female, but she still hasn't learned to act."

On the other hand Howard Barnes, on the *Herald Tribune*, had no such reaction. He called it "a superior item for connoisseurs of mayhem and love-making," saying that "it packs a mean melodramatic wallop," and as for the leading lady, "Miss Bacall . . . handles herself professionally, and has some startling dialogues with Bogart as they fence romantically."

Barnes may not have been confused, but he was about the only one. Sometime after the general release Bogart was on his boat, and two men from a nearby boat recognized him and came over in their dinghy. "Hey," one of them called, "what happened to the chauffeur?" (A chauffeur in the picture had vanished, and had never been referred to again.)

"I'm damned if I know," was all that Bogart could tell him.

In spite of the confusion the picture was a solid success, and the Bogart-Bacall team gladdened the hearts of the gnomes in the Accounting Office.

Bogart was then loaned to Columbia to do a picture called *Dead Reckoning*, the only noteworthy item about it being the fact that he asked for John Cromwell, his friend and riding companion who had directed him so long ago in *Swifty*, to be the director. Cromwell was then at RKO, but he came to Columbia and did the picture, which reverberated with echoes of *The Maltese Falcon* and *The Big Sleep*. It was, although not exactly a private-eye picture, in that same genre, with what was for that period an almost excessive amount of violence. It reinforced the private-eye image, just as the gangster pictures had done to his image of a decade before.

The next item was an almost unqualified disaster. Back in 1945 he had made a picture called *The Two Mrs. Carrolls*, costarring Barbara Stanwyck and based on a play by Martin Vale. In it he played a homicidal painter who poisons his first wife after he's through doing her portrait, and tries to do the same with his second wife. Warners kept the picture kicking around for two years (an unreleased picture is listed as an asset on the books, and the minute it's released it becomes a liability), and finally turned it loose on the public.

Bosley Crowther was beside himself with rage. "An incredible monstrosity," he thundered, "as wretched a stew of picture-making as has been dished up in many a moon. Most conspicuous of its embarrassments is the performance which Humphrey Bogart gives as the homicidal artist. . . . Mr. Bogart behaves in the ponderous fashion of a dead-panned American thug whose mother was horribly frightened by a robot built by Dr. Frankenstein . . . he goes through the whole repertory of a low-budget bogey-man." (When Crowther was feeling mean, no pun was too bad for him.)

Howard Barnes, however, liked it better than the stage version — although he had severe reservations about Miss Stanwyck — and he wrote that "Humphrey Bogart gives a brilliantly modulated performance as he gradually changes from a dashing suitor to a Borgia-like Van Gogh," thereby proving once and for all that one man's low-budget bogey-man is another man's brilliantly modulated performance.

He and Betty followed *The Big Sleep* with a picture called *Dark Passage*, which had the familiar innocent-man-trying-to-clear-himself theme. But it was well done, and it was a definite plus in a year that seesawed between the plus and the minus.

Early in 1947 Bogart went to Mexico with the Hustons, *père et fils*, to make *The Treasure of the Sierra Madre.* John Huston had done the screenplay, based on a novel by one B. Traven, an offbeat American who had holed up in Mexico and who came out of seclusion in order to be technical consultant. The company lived on location in the mountains, and the shooting schedule was a long one, but the end result more than justified the grueling work that went into it. For Bogart it was an entirely new character, that of an amiable bum who is turned into an animal by his lust for gold, and it was the start of a whole new phase in his career. When the picture opened, in January of the following year, Bosley Crowther atoned for his low-budget bogey-man remarks by writing that "physically, morally, and mentally, this character goes to pot before our eyes . . . the final appearance of him . . . is one to which few actors would lend themselves. Mr. Bogart's compensation should be the knowledge that his performance in this film is perhaps the best and most substantial that he has ever done." Taking a deep breath, he called the picture "a searching drama of the collision of civilization's vicious greeds with the instinct for self-preservation in the environment where all the barriers are down."

When Academy Award time came around, John won Oscars for Best Direction and Best Screenplay; his father, Walter, won the Best Supporting Actor award, and the film itself was nosed out of Best Picture by Laurence Olivier's *Hamlet*. Olivier also won in the Best Actor category. Bogart wasn't nominated, but his performance is still remembered in a film that has become a classic. And, of equal importance, it got him away from the private-eye image. Duke Mantee and Sam Spade were now behind him; he could branch out and do pretty much as he chose.

It was toward this end that he decided to set up his own company, and in 1947, with the help of Sam Jaffe and Mary Baker, he established the Santana Pictures Corporation, with himself as president and Robert Lord, a producer, as vice-president. It was the first time an actor had organized his own company, and Jack Warner was furious. He claimed that it was a menace to the industry that an actor should be allowed to make his own pictures; to him, anyone who upset the status quo was an enemy of the business, and he banned the Jaffe-Baker partners from the Warner lot. This made it impossible for them to get jobs at Warners for their other clients, and many of their clients left them, but both they and Bogart stood firm, and in the end Warner gave in because he couldn't fight it. In all, Santana made four pictures, released through Columbia, and one with Romulus Productions, released through United Artists. The last picture Bogart did for Warners was *Chain Lightning*, in 1950, and he terminated his contract shortly thereafter.

The one other item of importance that happened in 1947 was more in the political than the motion-picture field. The first frost was forming on what was becoming known as the Cold War, and the politicians were beginning to explore the possibilities of anti-Communism as a vote-getting device. McCarthy and Nixon were not yet prominently involved and the scare tactics had not begun, but in October J. Parnell Thomas and his House Committee on Un-American Activities decided to take a look at Hollywood and see if they could discern any Communist subversion in the motion-picture business.

They found that someone had tried to make Mickey Mouse squeak the Party line, and they found that Ayn Rand was alarmed by the sight of happy Russian children, and they found a few similar bits of trivia from cooperative witnesses. (One of these, a columnist, is reported, following his testimony, to have seen W. C. Fields on a golf course and, when he asked Fields if he could join him, received the reply: "Hell, no — if I'm going to play with a prick I'm going to play with my own.") Then nineteen writers, directors, and producers formed a bloc and took the position that it was none of the committee's business what their affiliations were or ever had been, and they would not cooperate. Of the nineteen eleven were called, and one (Bertolt Brecht) fled to East Germany; the remaining ten refused to answer, using the freedom of speech guaranteed by the First Amendment rather than the self-incrimination clause in the Fifth. John Huston gathered together a planeload of stars and other luminaries to go to Washington in support of the so-called "Unfriendly Ten," and the Bogarts were prominent among these junketeers.

Then it began to appear that the Communist Party was purposely making martyrs of the Ten — or, if not actively directing them, at least profiting from their martyrdom — and Bogart, feeling that he was being used, backed away from the whole thing. Others in Huston's group felt that he'd ducked the issue, but the simple fact was he wanted no part of something that involved him in matters beyond his control. He pulled out, and had nothing further to do with politics until 1952, when Betty got him involved in the Adlai Stevenson campaign. (His first dip into politics had been in November of 1944, when he made a radio speech endorsing Franklin D. Roosevelt for reelection. He received a great deal of denunciatory mail, the main tenor of it being that actors shouldn't have opinions like other people, and he wrote a reply in a piece called "I Stuck My Neck Out," which ex–brother-in-law Stuart Rose, then editor of the *Saturday Evening Post*, ran in the magazine. The thrust of his piece was that he would continue to speak out whenever he felt like it.)

The Ten were convicted of contempt of Congress and when, almost two years later, the Supreme Court by a five to four decision refused to hear their appeal, they went to jail for terms ranging up to a year. Those who went to

His third and final skirmish with politics: at the Un-American Affairs hearing
on the so-called "Unfriendly Ten." Others in the picture are Danny Kaye
and June Havoc, standing, and Betty, seated.

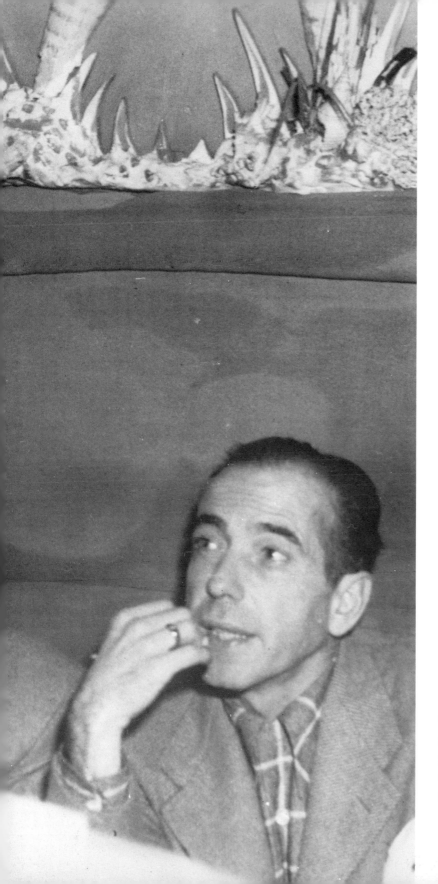

The paternity party the
night Steve was born. Left
to right are Sinatra, Dave
Chasen, Paul Douglas, and
the haggard father.

the Federal Correctional Institution in Danbury, Connecticut, were cheered by the sight of fellow-inmate J. Parnell Thomas, doing a stretch for taking kickbacks.

As for Bogart, he went back to making movies. He and Betty continued their husband-and-wife act in *Key Largo*, directed by John Huston and adapted by Huston and Richard Brooks from the play by Maxwell Anderson. It was a more familiar role for Bogart than the *Sierra Madre* one; the play, in fact, had some of the overtones of *The Petrified Forest*, except that this time Bogart was the disillusioned idealist and Edward G. Robinson represented the forces of evil. Anderson's play had been set in 1939, following the Spanish Civil War, and Huston and Brooks updated and expanded the story to the point where Bosley Crowther thought there was too much talk, but Otis L. Guernsey, Jr., who succeeded Howard Barnes on the *Herald Tribune*, called it "a bowstring-tight humdinger of movie make-believe."

It was, although nobody knew it at the time, the last picture he and Betty would make together; to her great delight she became pregnant, and her attention was diverted to more immediate and mundane matters than movie make-believe.

Bogart's first reaction to his upcoming fatherhood was one of shock. He had been married almost without letup for twenty-three years and the thought of children had, apparently, never been considered; now, nearing fifty years old, at the height of his career, and married to the one woman who made him truly happy (and was becoming adept as an acting partner), a foreign element had been introduced and it was, as the sportscasters say, a new ball game. It took a while for him to readjust to the fact that he was going to have to share Betty with someone else, but in the end he made the transition without undue grief. Once he accepted the situation, in fact, he rather liked it.

In this he had the help and support of his friends. Once the word was out, the event was anticipated like an Academy Award evening, and as the time drew near the preparations in some quarters were little short of feverish. A group of his friends — Mike Romanoff, Sinatra, Paul Douglas, and others — gave

September 29, 1949 — Bogie on the morning following the so-called Panda Affair,
when a model named Robin Roberts charged him with assault for having shoved
her when she tried to take his panda away from him at El Morocco. He
maintained, correctly, that the panda belonged to his son Stevie, and that Miss
Roberts had no right to it. She claimed to be able to show bruises proving
he used excessive force in protecting his son's panda. General apathy ensued.

Bogart a baby shower; they brought presents for him and took him out on the town, and when, in the tiny hours of the morning, they brought him home, he was clutching to his breast an assortment of baby shoes, dresses, and diapers, holding them as tenderly as if the baby were swaddled among them.

He went with Betty the night she was taken to the hospital, but his presence did little or nothing to help matters. This was a time when it was considered A Good Thing for the husband to be in the delivery room, to hold his wife's hand and witness the birth of their offspring, but Bogie didn't understand the medical terms and he couldn't bear to see anyone suffer, and he turned a sickly green at the whole idea and had to be taken out and revived with martinis. When, in the course of time, a son was born, he was named Steve (Betty's name for Bogie in *To Have and Have Not*), and the exhausted father tottered out and was feted by friends.

While Betty was in the hospital it snowed — an unusual, but by no means unheard-of thing in southern California — and when she brought five-day-old Steve home the ground was covered to a depth of three inches. As they came up the driveway they were confronted by a snowman on the lawn, which Bogie had laboriously packed together as a welcome-home present to his son. If Betty had any lingering doubts as to his attitude about fatherhood this went a long way toward dispelling them, as did what she heard on the intercom a few days later. They had an intercom between Steve's room and their own, so as to be able to hear if he made any noise in the night, and Betty, lying in bed, heard Bogie stop in the nursery as he left the house on his way to work. Then she heard small bits of baby talk, and words like, "Hey, fella — hello, little fella," and she knew that Duke Mantee had become a father. He would have died of mortification if he knew he'd been heard.

For a man who cried at weddings, Bogart went to considerable lengths to conceal the softer side of his nature. He was sentimental about presents and he tended to break up at all sorts of things, but he would cover it with a smirk or a sneer if other people were present, and would do his best to appear unmoved. A casual passerby might get the impression that he never even looked at his children (a daughter, Leslie Howard, was born in 1952), but Sammy Cahn, the songwriter and their neighbor when they moved to Holmby Hills, would occasionally see him through the foliage, playing with them on their swings and doing what he could to share their fun. It was a tricky business; with a half-century head start he couldn't be really close, but he put out a hand whenever he could. Sometimes they mystified him, as in the time when the swimming pool was being filled by a hose, and Steve had shrieking hysterics at the thought that the pool might overflow and the hose keep on running and drown them all. It was an odd phobia, and Bogart was flabbergasted that a son of his could have had such a reaction. He stood back as though Steve were juggling hand grenades, and let somebody else try to do the soothing.

Leslie, who wore bangs and Chinese smocks and had immense, round eyes, was as beautiful and as silent as a porcelain figurine, and if she didn't share her brother's temperament she did share his inheritance of their mother's features. In a contemplative mood, Bogart could take pride in the fact that, for one who had started so late as a father, he had come out so spectacularly

Seven-week-old Steve, looking understandably apprehensive as his father wields the diaper pins.

The Bogart family in June 1954, when Steve was five and Leslie one and a half.

well. (Another late-starting father, John O'Hara, was astounded that any offspring of his could wind up with the correct number of heads, and this appeared to be a common feeling among those who had stood on the sidelines for any length of time.)

He was good with children, but there were signs that they occasionally made him nervous. (As he remarked to screenwriter Peter Viertel: "It's easy to be good with *other* people's kids.") Back when he was married to Mary Philips, she and he were godparents to John and Eleanor Halliday's son John, and once when the youth was in town on vacation from prep school Bogart offered to buy him a lunch. His mother was taking him to a matinee so it had to be an early lunch, and she delivered him to Bogart in the lobby of "21" at twelve-thirty sharp. Before she could leave, Bogart came darting after her and said, "For God's sake, what do you talk to a thirteen-year-old boy about?"

"You're his godfather," she replied. "You're supposed to be in charge of his religious instruction."

Later, when she and her son were in a cab on the way to the theater, she asked him what he and his godfather had talked about.

"Not much," John replied. "He said, 'Listen, kid, there are twelve Commandments,' and then he ordered a drink."

Betty was mildly amused when she heard the anecdote, but she pointed out that he knew every one of the Ten Commandments by heart, so it must have been either his or young John's nervousness that confused the count. Furthermore, she said, he made the Commandments his code, and while he seldom if ever set foot in a church he was still a deeply religious man. He had his own code, and his own way of life, and there was nothing in the world that could change it. As an example of this immutability, she cited the time when they were at Sinatra's in Palm Springs with the Romanoffs; Sinatra wanted them to stay on and the Romanoffs agreed, but Bogie wanted to go, so they left. When they were in the car he said, "This is Frank's way; he's chosen this kind of . . . footloose life for himself, but we have our own lives. We have our own way of living, and we don't have to live anybody else's way of life." And that was that.

Bogart was also protective, not only of his family but also of others who were either lonely or lost or out of luck, or for whom he felt responsible. He used the "Which way is Hollywood?" test for any departing guest who he felt might have trouble with the police, and if the guest couldn't point immediately toward Hollywood (which was the Beverly Hills police way of separating the drunk from the sober) Bogart insisted he be driven home by someone with either less alcohol or a better sense of direction. Generally speaking, a newcomer in Hollywood does not get invited to a party unless he is already at one; the spare-guest lists are made up of those who have proven themselves presentable in public, and the telephone is used only as a last resort, but Bogart was bound by no such ritual. If he knew someone who was recently arrived or alone, he would call with an informal invitation such as, "A few people are coming by for drinks," or, "What are you doing for dinner?" or, more simply, "Get your ass over here," and that would be the invitation. (Another way in which it differed from the norm was that the host did the calling; the usual routine is to give the lucky invitee your unlisted phone number, with the exhortation to "drop around any time next week — but call before you come.") One time in London, Adolph Green, Betty Comden's collaborator, knew that the Bogarts were in town and, although he didn't know them very well, called their hotel to say hello. Bogart not only said hello, he invited Green to have dinner with them — a dinner at which the other two guests turned out to be Vivien Leigh and Laurence Olivier. He continued to check with Green thereafter, not only in London but also in Hollywood, to make sure he was being properly fed and cared for. He even, at one point, made the superlative hostly gesture of trying to arrange him a bit of bed life, but somebody changed the subject and the idea was forgotten. (This was just as well, because the whole thing was most certainly a gag, and if it had been carried through he would have been shocked and upset. The Puritan in him was never very far beneath the surface.)

His protectiveness also entered into his profession. He felt that actors were

Eric Hatch, photographed by Bogart. Bogart claimed Hatch
was a worse ham than any actor.

Gertie then Hatch now Chase, for whom the Sporting Syndicate was allegedly formed.

Eric Hatch, author of the novel and screenplay *My Man Godfrey,* in his last Rolls Royce, the one he coasted as often as possible to save gasoline.

Bogie had a photographic dark room in the Horn Avenue house, where he and Eric Hatch made occasional photo-montages, such as the one above. The identification of the skier and the owner of the mammary are unknown. Another montage put the face of a cat, belonging to Bogie's sister Pat, on Mel Baker's head, with a result that was not wholly satisfying.

always being used — by requests to perform, or appear, or donate their talents to one cause or another — and he encouraged them to hold out and not demean their work by giving it away for nothing. When the television version of *The Petrified Forest* was being cast, he suggested Natalie Schafer for the part of Mrs. Chisolm, one of those taken hostage by the gangsters. Miss Schafer's agent asked a sum that made the producer choke; negotiations bogged down, and because she wanted the part Miss Schafer was about to lower her sights. At that point Bogart called her, told her he wanted her in the play, and said she should stand fast on her price. Heartened by his support she did stand fast, and she got it.

There was another, totally different area where his protectiveness operated. Back in 1938 Eric Hatch fell on lean times, and Bogart decided he needed some money to help him through the trouble. Aware of the delicate nature of the proposal, he organized what was called "The Sporting Syndicate," in which he and Mel Baker and Allen Rivkin and Elliot Nugent and a writer named Leonard Lee banded together to see what they could do to help. They arranged to meet Hatch by the Brown Derby, on Wilshire Boulevard, and at the appointed time they saw him wheeling down the boulevard in an old Rolls Royce. He approached them in stately grandeur, and it began to look as though he didn't need their help after all, until they realized that for the last few blocks he'd been coasting — "to save gas," as he explained. (There was a small downgrade in the road at that point.) Bogart outlined their mission, and Hatch said he was all right — he needed nothing — but his voice wasn't very steady and Bogart sensed an emotional scene coming on, so he turned tough. "Listen, you dumb fuck," he snarled, "we're not doing this for you, we're doing it for Gertie. How much do you need?" Hatch allowed as how five thousand dollars would see him through,* and Bogart turned to the others and told them to get up their share. Nugent said he'd have to talk to his business manager, so Bogart guaranteed the balance, and the money was paid through *his* business manager, Morgan Maree.

St. Bernard de Clairvaux (1091–1153) in his *Sermo Primus* first enunciated

---

* That is the figure as Rivkin remembers it. Hatch's then wife, now Mrs. Gertrude Chase, swears it was no more than six hundred dollars.

the truism: "Who loves me will love my dog also." Bogart wasn't too concerned about who loved him, but anyone who did anything against his dogs was courting a terrible retribution. At one point the Bogarts had two boxers, probably the most affectionate of animals but also inclined on occasion to give tongue, and in the course of time one of the neighbors complained to the police. (This man had been a member of a warmhearted comedy team, but his warmth apparently chilled a bit in retirement.) Bogart's rage was incandescent. "The son of a bitch doesn't like *dogs!*" he shouted. "What kind of monster is he? The barking of dogs is a *cheerful* sound — he ought to be *glad* he can hear them!" Then, totally by coincidence, when Bogart was in the hospital this ex-comedian, who wanted to make some changes on his property, went among the others in the area with a petition (local ordinance said two-thirds of the neighborhood must agree to any significant change). When Bogart returned from the hospital he found that his friend Sammy Cahn had signed, and he was outraged. "Don't you remember that bastard hates dogs?" he said. "How could you sign anything for a goddamned dog hater?" Cahn pointed out that *he* hadn't had any valid complaint, but Bogart wasn't mollified. Later that night he called Cahn, and said, "I just thought. Were there any witnesses when you signed that petition?"

"No," Cahn replied. "He was alone."

"Then it's not legal," Bogart said, and hung up.

To his wife, Cahn said, "You know something? I think Bogie's going to get well."

(As a footnote, Art Linkletter, another neighbor, has written that a lot of people were upset by the Bogarts' dogs, but that they decided against any drastic action because of the publicity it would have involved. The most they managed to do, according to Linkletter, was to get Bogart to keep the dogs indoors at night.)

Betty says firmly that he was never intentionally cruel to anyone — that his targets were the pompous or the stuffy or the phony, and that doesn't constitute cruelty — and while there are people who might argue that point, she is in the position of being the one who should know. She says he learned a valuable lesson once when he was a young actor, in the office of David Belasco, who had in front of him a script that was little short of rancid. The author came in, and Belasco gave him a long spiel that involved such phrases as "some awfully good points," "a great deal to be said for it," "a little more work here and there," "touch up this scene a bit," and so on, and when the writer had left, Bogart asked why all the soft soap — why hadn't he come right out and said the script stunk?

"When you see a person who's done his best and it's no good," Belasco replied, "then you can't be cruel. If you know he can do better, then you say it stinks and he should get with it, but when you know this is the best he can do, just be gentle."

If Bogart dissembled about his sentimentality, he made no attempt to hide his feelings about honesty and integrity. When he and Betty were married he told her they must always be honest with each other; he was aware of the difference in their ages, and he said that if she ever found someone she preferred she should tell him, and if he thought the man would be good for her he'd step aside and let her go. At one point she became fascinated by Leonard Bernstein, and while Bogart was aware of it he neither said nor did anything; it wasn't in his makeup to play the jealous or suspicious husband. When Betty told him Bernstein was coming out to California and would be there for the weekend, he said, "I can't stand all that piano playing — sitting around on the floor — I'm going off on the boat." And he went, leaving her to listen to the piano.

And, lest there should be any misinterpretation of the above, we will let her speak for herself: "Lenny Bernstein was never a threat to my marriage. He was only a part of my growing up and continued exposure to talented, exciting people. Bogie and Lenny were fond of each other and I want no inference that a romance might have been going on." Anyone who knew her knows she would never have dallied while married, but it's just as well the record be straight. There is an actor/director who once, many years ago, took

176

a low-grade pass at her, and his ears are still ringing from the rebuff. He'd have done better if he'd walked into a whirling airplane propeller. To sum up on Bernstein, she says: ". . . there was excitement as there always is with music for me; it was someone so completely involved with his work — so active — that in California in particular it was like a strong wind."

The Puritan in Bogart, referred to parenthetically a while back, was a force of major proportions. His dislike of off-color jokes has already been mentioned, and the odd fact is that, despite the occasional gamy epithets that studded his talk, his language was generally of the drawing-room variety. He could turn the obscenities on or off like a faucet; they were not the crutch for him that they are for people with more limited vocabularies. If the obscenities were superficial the Puritan was deeply ingrained, and he could become a finger-shaking moralist at a moment's notice. When he was in Italy making *The Barefoot Contessa* he ran across Ingrid Bergman, whose romance with Roberto Rossellini had scandalized the DAR and other self-righteous elements in this country, and he berated her for having thrown away her career in such a fashion.

"You were the top of the heap," he concluded. "You were a great star, and now look at you. What are you now?"

"A happy woman," she replied.

Next to Betty, his great love was the boat; he was, purely and simply, a boat nut. When Ernest Hemingway's *The Old Man and the Sea* appeared in *Life* he read it, then passed the magazine to Betty. "Read that," he said. "That's how I feel." Hemingway had written that the old man "knew that no man was ever alone on the sea," and that the sea was the only place where a man could be really free.

In 1941, when he was married to Mayo, he and she used to cruise the coast-line together in his cabin cruiser *Sluggy*, and sometimes make the twenty-mile trip to Santa Catalina Island, but there wasn't a great deal of pleasure cruising during the war, and *Sluggy* never became the glorious escape hatch that the later and larger yawl *Santana* did. Like many eager and patriotic boat owners, Bogart signed up with the Coast Guard Inshore Patrol after Pearl Harbor, and *Sluggy* made periodic — and futile — antisubmarine patrols. It's probably just well she never tangled with a Japanese submarine, although if Mayo had been on board the battle would at least have been a close one. The nearest *Sluggy* ever came to action was once when, running out of San Pedro Harbor, she passed a group of Navy destroyers at anchor; a lookout recognized Bogart, and the destroyer's guns swiveled around and tracked him as he went past. Others picked it up, and Bogie ran the line of ships staring into the black muzzles of batteries of five-inch guns.

Santana was something else again. She was named after the wind that blows

Santana under way.

Betty learning the ropes, a knowledge that faded with lack of use.

out of the desert, which properly spelled is Santa Ana, and one time, in a half-serious discussion of the unlikely event of financial disaster, he said, "No matter what happens, the boat goes last." *Santana* was mother, wife, and mistress to him, and if Betty seldom ventured aboard it could be argued that she knew competition when she saw it, and wanted no part of it. (To be perfectly honest boats bored her rigid, a reaction shared by many people who can see no point in sitting canted over to one side all day, having spray blown in their face.)

For a sailing enthusiast, however, *Santana* was fifty-four feet of pure delight. The master cabin, in the stern, slept two; the main cabin had folding transoms that could sleep two or even four more, and then forward of the galley was sleeping space for two — the boat captain and on occasion a cook, who was an off-duty fireman from San Diego. The plumbing facilities were adequate if not spacious, although on an all-male weekend they received limited use — as Bogie once said: "The trouble with having dames along is you can't pee over the side." Except on the Fourth of July, when there was an annual bring-your-ladies regatta to Catalina, the sailing weekends were all male, and the etiquette informal to a degree. But the boat was always spotless. An observer once remarked that at home Bogie was the kind who left his clothes where he stepped out of them, and that Betty had to pick up after him and remind him when to shave, but on the boat everything was in its place and everything glistened. You might not have to shave, but you damn well didn't clutter up the boat, and if you got anything dirty you cleaned it.

And, on the subject of the July Fourth regatta, David Niven and his wife Hjördis were once the invited guests. In his highly engaging memoirs *The Moon's a Balloon*, he tells how they went to Catalina and were joined by Sinatra on a chartered yacht, and how Sinatra sang literally all through the night, while people from other yachts paddled over in their dinghies and rubber boats and floated in a quiet circle around *Santana*. There was a full moon, and the spell wasn't broken until, when daylight began to tint the sky, the singing ended, and the people paddled away.

The sailing weekends began about ten o'clock Saturday morning, when Bogie left home in his small, black Mercedes and headed down Sepulveda Boulevard for the hour-long drive to Newport Harbor. He became visibly more relaxed as he drove, and by the time he nosed the car into the corrugated iron shed on the waterfront there might have been three thousand miles between him and Hollywood. *Santana* was alongside the dock nearby, with the boat captain, Carl Petersen, waiting in attendance. Petersen, although Danish, was referred to by the skipper as "Kraut," "Square-head," "Pete," "Dum Bum," or any one of a number of epithets, and he answered to all of them with equal cheerfulness. (It was an interesting thing about Bogart that he could use ethnic nicknames without giving offense. He often called Sinatra "the Dago," something that might earn anyone else a pair of broken arms. To him, Sinatra's reaction was a gentle smile.)

As soon as he stepped aboard he poured himself a Scotch, then put the glass in a holder near the binnacle. (*Santana* probably had more glass holders per square foot of deck space than any other boat in the area.) The engine was started, the lines taken in, and the boat nosed out into the stream. The matter of hoisting and setting the sails required a lot of work, but if the guests were at all adept it could be done in fairly short order. Jeff Richards and Dewey Martin, two young actors who often accompanied him, were as well trained as any professional crew, and they leaped about like photogenic apes under the critical eye of the skipper. Once the sails were up and the course was set, he would give the helm to someone else, and his relaxation would be complete.

The trip across took from three to five hours, depending on the wind and tide. Catalina is a hilly, barren island about eighteen miles long, inhabited primarily by goats. Avalon, a resort town on the southern end, has a casino and a variety of tourist attractions, and there are air and ferry connections with the mainland, but once away from Avalon you might as well be in the mountains of Greece. As a matter of fact, a movie company long ago used the island as location for a picture about Greece, and the temple columns they built stood for a long time after the picture was forgotten. The main attraction of Catalina, as far as the sailing fraternity is concerned, is the getting there.

Carl Petersen, otherwise known as "Kraut," "Pete," "Dum Bum," and "Squarehead." The sight of him in a red fright wig with pigtails made strong men faint.

Santana moored at Cherry Cove, Catalina.

Santana would use an anchorage in Cherry Cove, north of Avalon, where the water was clear and the beach accessible, and there was the company of other sailors and yachtsmen. There was swimming for those who were so minded, or for that matter any other simple recreation, but the first order of business was always for Petersen to take the dinghy and set out the lobster traps. Since lobstering in the area was illegal he was technically poaching, and in deference to the law he didn't use the regular type of pot buoy; he tied an empty gin bottle on a long line to each trap. Then, later that evening or early next morning, he would make a round of the bobbing gin bottles, haul the traps, and take what was inside. Sometimes the catch was nothing but a baby shark or two, but more often there were a few *langoustes*, the clawless Pacific lobsters. They would be hustled aboard, and their tails wrenched off and dropped in boiling water as quickly as possible. The sharks were killed, on general principles.

In the field of aquatic sports, Jeff Richards and Dewey Martin once went on a water-skiing jaunt that came within inches of being a first-class marine disaster. They took *Santana*'s outboard motorboat and, with Richards on the skis, Martin in the bow for balance, and a third man running the motor, they set off for the open water outside the anchorage. They zoomed about for a while, cutting the usual water-skiing capers, and then on one turn Richards fell off. The boat lurched forward with the lessening of the drag, and the man at the motor, who'd been sitting up on the stern, fell backward into the water. Martin, who was looking forward, was unaware of what had happened, and the watchers on *Santana* were transfixed to see him, alone in the bow, speeding toward anchorage, while two heads bobbed in the wake far astern. Nobody could hear anything, but they saw Martin apparently say something over his shoulder, wait a moment, say it again, then turn and frantically scramble over the seats and grab the controls, just in time to avoid smashing into the crowded anchorage. There was a good deal of laughter about it later, but very little at the time. It was like seeing a slow-motion picture of a train wreck, unable to do anything about it.

On another trip young Stevie Bogart, then six or seven years old, came along as a nonworking member of the crew. For some reason he felt it important to

184

bring an empty cricket cage, and while his father didn't see the point in it he didn't object. ("One word from me and he does as he pleases," was the way he explained his relationship with Stevie.) When it came time for lobstering, Stevie decided he wanted to catch a lobster in his cricket cage (an obvious impossibility, since the cage was one-third the size of a mature lobster), and to that end he hung it on a string over the stern. He inspected it every ten minutes, after sunset with the aid of a flashlight, and he was persuaded to go to bed only after he'd dropped the light in the water. It could be seen, glowing faintly, about twenty-five feet down, and Stevie had no choice but to wait until morning. The adults had a few rounds of drinks before dinner, then afterward cleared the table, broke out the Drambuie, and began to play dominoes. For a long time there was quiet, broken only by a muttered "Shee-it," from a player, and then one of them stood up.

"I'm going to get that flashlight," he announced, and began to take off his clothes. He stripped to his shorts and went on deck, while the others gleefully followed, making bets as to whether or not he'd succeed. He dove over the side and swam down, groping his way toward the shimmering circle of light, and although he swam for what seemed like an eternity he wasn't able to reach it. Finally, with his lungs bursting and his ears clogged, he clawed his way upward to fresh air, luckily not skulling himself on *Santana*'s keel.

"You never got beneath the surface!" Bogie shouted, laughing. "Your feet are still in the air!"

The man, for whom idiot is too soft a word, gulped a few times and then went down again, but got no closer to the light than before. He pulled himself aboard to the well-earned jeers of the others, and had a warming drink while drying himself. It was then that Bogie decided, as a joke on Steve, to put the fore part of a lobster in his cricket cage, and see his reaction next morning. That done, the company had another drink and then retired.

Stevie's shouts, when he spied the lobster thorax in his cage, woke everyone including the recent diver, who spent the rest of the day in the clutches of a raging, man-eating hangover. Apparently the water pressure had force-fed the Scotch and Drambuie into his bloodstream, thereby trebling its effect, and all he could do was lie quietly in the shade, waiting for death. Every time he rolled over liquid seeped from one aperture or another; every time he tried to stand he became dizzy, and sitting up brought on a desire to lie down. During the entire return trip he lay sprawled across the cabin trunk, periodically oozing Drambuie. Bogart, at the wheel, observed him sourly.

"I'm certainly glad we brought *you* along," he said, at last. "You've been a big addition to the party."

The afternoon was made even more hideous by the sudden appearance, through the hatch, of Petersen, grinning broadly and wearing a red fright wig with long pigtails. Bogart shouted, "Jesus Christ Almighty!" and then Petersen sank slowly out of sight, leaving the ship's company speechless and shaken.

When I went out to California to work on a picture (and again, there seems no way to avoid the first person here), I had just finished a biography of my father, and was all full of the material. Just once too often, I said, "A funny thing happened to my father —" and Bogie spun on me.

"Oh, shut up about your father," he said. "You're out here on your own, not on your father. Let's have no more talk about your father." I apologized, and the incident was apparently closed.

Later that day, as he was nosing *Santana* into the anchorage at Cherry Cove, he came close enough to another boat so that he introduced his crew to the others. "Right there is Dewey Martin," he said. "At the mast is Jeff Richards. And the tall man in the bow is Nat Benchley." Pause. "He's Sinclair Lewis's boy."

It was not always easy to find three men with time on their hands over a weekend — three men who liked to sail, that is — and Bogart was constantly looking for new members. One of them was David Niven, who in his book recalls that, when Bogart asked him if he liked to sail, he made the mistake of saying he'd done it all his life; had, in fact, represented his country in the eight-meter class. Bogart eyed him speculatively, and told him they'd go out on Sunday. They did, with a brisk wind, and at one point found themselves headed toward a group of tuna boats with long nets astern. Bogart held his course until the very last minute, then let go the wheel, grinned at Niven, and said, "Take over, big shot. I'm going to the can."

Luckily, Niven made the right move (out of three possibilities, only one was correct), and trouble was avoided. But it taught him you shouldn't boast to Bogart unless you were prepared to back it up.

The end of a boating weekend was always a letdown, with the long Sunday-afternoon drive and the knowledge of what lay ahead for the next five days. Once, when he pulled into a filling station for gas, he was served by a youth who clearly thought of himself as a budding star, or comic, or both. Noting Bogart's two-day growth of beard, he polished the windshield furiously, then chuckled and said, "We didn't stand very close to the razor this morning, did we?"

Bogart was too depressed to reply. He knew he was back in Hollywood.

T HE FOUR SANTANA FILMS released through Columbia were *Knock on Any Door*, *Tokyo Joe*, *In a Lonely Place*, and *Sirocco*, and there wasn't one of them that would warrant an actor-producer's saying, "Now do you see why I went off on my own?" It was faintly embarrassing, having split from Warners because he was tired of their trash, to be unable to come up with a truly distinguished picture, but one of the frustrating things about the movies is that the harder you try to be distinguished the more likely you are to fall on your face.

In 1935 one Cecil Scott Forester, an English medical-student-turned-writer, confected an adventure story called *The African Queen*, which told of a Cockney river rat and an English missionary's sister in the Belgian Congo during World War I. It was a wild tale of romance and of incredible hardships, as the pair took a small, rickety steamboat downstream to confront the enemy on Lake Wittelsbach, on the border of German Central Africa. Since it was a romance and since, during their journey, they had become sexually entangled (a spicy thought in 1935), the author deemed it best to have them get married in the end, in spite of the obvious difference in their backgrounds, social position, and general outlook. Acknowledging the improbability of such an arrangement, he ended the book with the sentence: "Whether or not they lived happily ever after is not easily decided." He then had his secretary type up the manuscript and send it to the publisher, and he turned to the writing of another book — or books; his next one was *The General,* and the one after that *Captain Horatio Hornblower.*

In the course of time, while he was immersed in one or the other of these works, he heard from the publishers that they were unhappy with his ending of *The African Queen,* but they thought they could fix it without any work from him, simply by lopping off the last two chapters and letting the reader decide for himself how it should end. This was fine with Forester, because the book had long since lost his interest, and it wasn't until he received his pre-publication copies that he realized the idea had been a mistake. He had to wait until 1940, when the book was reissued in a Modern Library edition, to rectify it and restore the two missing chapters.

The story kicked around the movie studios for several years, and nothing much was done about it. James Agee, the writer and sometime critic, hammered out a version that was not a shooting script but at least a starter, and in 1951 Sam Spiegel (otherwise known as S. P. Eagle) put together a deal that had Huston as the director and coscreenwriter, Bogart as Charlie Allnut the river rat (changed from Cockney to Canadian, and deprived of the double "t" with which Forester spelled the name), and Katharine Hepburn as the missionary's sister. The picture was shot in the spring and summer of 1951, in the then Belgian Congo.

The logistics for such a venture were on a scale reminiscent of the Allied invasion of Africa. Bogart was nagged by premonitions of disaster, but like everyone else who worked with Huston he was mesmerized by the director's personality, drive, and imagination, and he let himself be drawn into situations he would have considered insane in other circumstances. But this feeling that he had, of being in the first wave of a doomed amphibious operation, led him to make the most of the time he and Betty had in Paris on the way to Africa, and to wring every last ounce of enjoyment out of the hours remaining to him.

One example should suffice. The Bogarts, plus Huston, screenwriter Peter Viertel, Joan Fontaine and her escort, Prince Nicholas of Yugoslavia, were headed for lunch at the Méditerranée, one of Paris's more elegant eating places. On the way Bogart spied an old *clochard*, the French word for a grizzled wino (most of whom wear Basque berets), and, feeling that the party needed a democratic touch to offset the presence of royalty, he invited the *clochard* to join them. Bemused but not unwilling, the man agreed, and when they reached the restaurant a place was made for him at the table. The lunch was long, liquid, and moderately hilarious, and at the conclusion there were brandy and cigars. When, finally, the party was outside, Bogart gave the *clochard* an extra cigar and the French equivalent of fifty dollars, and thanked him for joining them. As they drove off they looked back and saw him stroll down the block, puffing his cigar with Edwardian aplomb, and finally, at the end of the block, stop and take the money from his pocket, and slowly count it. Bogart later picked up a *poule* whom he introduced as his fiancée, but that joke didn't go over so well. Everything considered, his batting average was better than might have been expected.

The company went down in fragments to what was then Stanleyville, capital of the Belgian Congo. Huston, insistent on finding a "black water" river, went first and scouted the area, and finally saw what he wanted in a tributary of the Congo River. When Bogart and Betty arrived, he greeted them with a broad smile and said, "Well, I've found it. We have almost every known kind of disease, and almost every known kind of serpent." He wasn't far wrong; Miss Hepburn subsequently found a poisonous black mamba snake in the ladies' loo, and by the time shooting was over everyone in the company except Bogart, Betty, and Huston had come down with some form of disease. Bogart, cheerfully ignoring Miss Hepburn's lectures about drinking, maintained a steady diet of baked beans, canned asparagus, and Scotch whiskey, and later claimed that whenever a fly bit him it dropped dead.

His premonitions of disaster came close to being realized. One day he and Betty and Viertel and Miss Hepburn decided to take a ride on the Congo in a small gasoline-driven launch, and the native boatman had trouble getting the engine started. After thoroughly flooding the carburetor he went below into the engine compartment and, in order to see better, lit a match. There was a flash, and a loud explosion, and the boatman, his skin and clothes on

With Betty and John Huston. The picture is not identified.

With Betty on location in *The African Queen*. The anti–mosquito/snakebite/antbite
medicine was always handy.

As Charles Allnut, in *The African Queen*, on his way to winning an Academy Awar

fire, came rocketing up and leaped over the side, where he tottered ashore and rolled in the sand. The launch, its engine smoking, began to drift downstream. Under Bogart's direction Viertel threw a line to a tied-up ship they were passing, then the crew of that ship passed across buckets of sand, with which Bogart went below and put out the fire. The boatman survived, and all hands were considered lucky in the extreme. Under the law of averages, the lot of them should have been blown up.

That wasn't their only trouble. The thirty-foot steam launch, a replica of the *African Queen*, had to be shipped by truck from Uganda; the truck got lost in the rainy season, and they had to go out looking for it in a small airplane. Then, subsequently, it sank. As Bogart described it: "We had some natives watching it, and they watched it until it sank right to the bottom of the river." It weighed ten tons, and since there were no cranes or derricks or other such equipment available, it had to be raised by hand. Everyone, including Betty, got on the lines and hauled, to the native chant of "Hoola HA!" and after two days of hoola-ha-ing they got it up. It took another day to put it back in operating order.

Their further problems, as told by Bogart to Art Buchwald, then a columnist for the Paris *Herald Tribune*, included an invasion by an army of soldier ants; labor trouble with the natives, who went on strike every payday (their pay was rice, fish, two cigarettes, and three shillings a day), an inconvenience that was mitigated only when someone hit on the idea of lengthening the time between paydays and thereby lessening the number of strikes; and a disastrous day when the trucks with the liquor supply didn't get through, and the entire company threatened to quit. Huston had a bottle hidden in an elephant-gun case (he was an avid big-game hunter), and that got him and Bogart through the night, but morale elsewhere was at a nadir.

Then there was the matter of the script. The ending, which had worried the publishers of the book, came back to haunt the moviemakers. In Forester's version, the *African Queen* had swamped in a storm before it could use its homemade torpedoes; its two occupants were taken aboard the German gunboat *Königen Luise*, were treated with courtesy by the captain, and under

With Betty and Katharine Hepburn, returning to London from the Congo and the shooting of *The African Queen*. His position on the step gives him an unnatural height advantage over the ladies.

a flag of truce were handed over to the British, who then sank the *Königen Luise* and released the lovers to go and find someone to marry them. The edited version ended with the German captain's deciding to be lenient, and that was all. Forester's version was too cluttered, and the edited version was too abrupt, so a whole new idea had to be developed. What finally emerged was a little bit of Forester and a little bit of Huston, plus a large dose of *deus ex machina*. The *African Queen* founders in a storm, Bogart and Hepburn are taken aboard the German ship *Louisa*, and the captain sentences them to be hanged as enemy agents. Bogart asks the captain to marry them before they die, and he does, but before they can be hanged the hulk of the *African Queen* sloshes up and the *Louisa* collides with it, setting off the torpedoes. Bogart and Hepburn are thrown clear by the explosion, and the picture ends with their paddling happily shoreward.

Sam Spiegel, the producer, visited the location twice during the shooting. He came down in a chartered yacht, wearing safari costume and bringing a retinue of servants and such conveniences as bottled water (the bottles, it turned out, were filled with tap water), but somehow he didn't really fit in the scene, and he soon gave up.

Vowing never to set foot in Africa again, Bogart returned to Paris in a less devil-may-care mood than when he'd left. He filled Buchwald in on his experiences, and then, in the car taking Buchwald back to the *Tribune*, he slumped down in the seat and said, "You know, the good thing about the French is they don't give a damn whether you're an actor or what. You can walk along the street here, and nobody even recognizes you." The car stopped at a light, and a Frenchman on the sidewalk looked in the window, made a pistol with his fingers and pointed it at Bogart, said, "*Boum, boum*," and walked away, laughing.

If he wanted anonymity in Paris, he got more than enough of it in Brooklyn, where he went one night on a personal-appearance tour of the Loew's theaters to plug the about-to-be-released *African Queen*. It was a Wednesday night and the movie houses were sparsely attended, and the United Artists publicity people were afraid that Bogart would be upset by lack of an audience. His act consisted of a few words about the picture, a few in praise of Miss Hepburn, and then he sang a ditty about a frog, and went off.* A routine like this might go in a crowded house, but before fifty or a hundred people it would take a grim toll on the man who performed it. So, as a diversionary tactic, the United Artists people gave five hundred dollars to a young man named Bob Condon to heckle Bogart into such a rage that he would be unaware of the empty seats. This Condon did, so successfully that Bogart almost exterminated him, and it was only at the end of the evening that Bogart was told the truth. He had been in such a rage that he had literally thought of nothing except getting rid of Condon, but when he learned the story he laughed, and took him to "21." Condon had earned every dime of his five hundred dollars.

The picture opened in New York on February 21, 1952, and Bosley Crowther of the *Times* called it "a slick job of hoodwinking with a thoroughly implausible romance." Of the male star, he wrote that "Bogart, in what is very likely the best performance of his long career, plays a man who is crude only on the surface; there is a goodness underneath his unshaven appearance, and the actor does a fine job of bringing this quality out in the action and dialogue."

So fine a job, in fact, that he was nominated for an Academy Award, as was Huston for the screenplay and the direction. The picture became one of the top money-makers of 1952.

It seemed, when the Academy nominations were announced, that *The African Queen* was bound to run second to the other highly successful picture, *A Streetcar Named Desire.* Four of *Streetcar*'s players were nominated: Marlon Brando for Best Actor, Vivien Leigh for Best Actress, Kim Hunter for Best Supporting Actress, and Karl Malden for Best Supporting Actor, and the picture itself carried with it the prestige of Tennessee Williams's Pulitzer Prize–winning play. Still there was no harm in hoping, and when people

* The frog song has been lost, although it is conceivable it was the same one performed on occasion by John Steinbeck, which went: "Got no ears,/Got no tail,/But I can hop-hop-hop,/And I can say Huack-Huack-Huack."

asked Bogart what he would say if he got the Oscar he replied, "I'm not going to thank anyone; I'm just going to say I damn well deserve it." Richard Brooks, the writer-director, suggested that if he got it he should look around, pause, then say, "It's about time." There were a lot of jokes on this order, but nobody really expected it to happen. The early straw polls showed *Streetcar* making a clean sweep.

This seemed to be confirmed the night of the Awards. Malden, Miss Hunter, and Miss Leigh all won in their categories, and when Greer Garson opened the Best Actor envelope it might have been expected that Brando was halfway out of his chair. But she read Bogart's name instead, and the house exploded. Stunned, he jogged up onto the stage, took the Oscar as gently as though it were a newborn baby, and said, "It's a long way from the Belgian Congo to the stage of the Pantages, but it's a lot nicer here." He then thanked Huston and Miss Hepburn for all they'd done for him, and retired to the wings. So much for the new kind of acceptance speech.

With the enlargement of the family Betty decided it was time they moved to a bigger house, and she found what she wanted at 232 Mapleton Drive in Holmby Hills. This is a bosky area between Beverly Hills and Bel Air, where Sunset Boulevard stops being straight and begins to snake its way through the hills toward the Pacific. The house, a long, two-story, white brick structure, was almost hidden from the street by heavy foliage, and the impression on entering the driveway was that of entering a forest glade. Behind the main building, a well-tended lawn sloped down to the swimming pool and patio; there was a tennis court, and an area for the children's slide and jungle gym and whatnot. In spite of — or perhaps because of — the size of the house, most of the living was done in the library, a paneled room with bookcases, a bar, comfortable chairs, folding tables on which meals were served, and a screen that could be let down for the showing of movies. The projector was set up in an adjoining toilet, with a small, removable panel in the wall. There was a large, formal living room, but it was never fully furnished; Bogie argued that they wouldn't use it except for big parties, and then they'd have caterers who could bring their own chairs. Any sensation of formality made him uneasy, and he did what he could to keep things simple. A lanai, furnished with wrought-iron tables and chairs, completed the downstairs living area. The kitchen was large and well supplied, and was open to any guest who, late at night, felt like concocting something to eat. Sinatra used on occasion to throw together an Italian specialty of his own or of his mother's, but this was only by whim or sudden impulse; if someone suggested that he do it, he lost interest. And, on the subject of Sinatra: Betty believes that he was fascinated by Bogie not only for the obvious reasons, but also because it intrigued him that Bogie could be a solid, well-organized family man and at the same time a *bon vivant* and the center of attention and not, as she put it, screw up somewhere along the way. The two characteristics don't often go together.

According to Sammy Cahn, Mapleton Drive during the 1940s had been a quiet, respectable street, with people like Donald Nelson, of the War Production Board; a gentleman named Gianini, of the Bank of America (to whom Cahn once went "to borrow a cup of money"); and assorted oil magnates and businessmen; and then, gradually, a more raffish element began to seep in, from that alien and unsubstantial world of entertainment. Bing Crosby, Art Linkletter, Judy Garland and Sid Luft, Lana Turner and Bob Topping, and finally, to cap it off, the Bogarts moved into what Cahn calls "a Judge Hardy house," and the revolution was complete. Cahn had the feeling that Bogart was miscast in the house, but if he was he never gave any indication of it. If it was a pleasure for Betty that was all that mattered, and if the more substantial neighbors objected to occasional noisy evenings — as, for instance, when Sinatra conducted a chorus of producers in a rendition of "Silent Night" — then they knew where they could go.

His dedication to Betty's happiness worked in every direction, from the major areas down to the wholly trivial ones. As an example of the latter, one evening when *Casablanca* was being shown in the library a friend offered to tend the projector, and after putting on the last reel closed the toilet door and joined the audience. (Betty had earlier, during the flashback-to-Paris scenes, said in a stage whisper, "Look how Y-O-U-N-G he looks," a twitting that received no reply.) At the end of the picture the volunteer projectionist returned to the toilet to take off the reel and found, to his horror, that he'd moved the projector just enough so that the lower spool had touched the wall and therefore stopped, and the entire toilet was a mass of squirming coils upon coils upon coils of film. Sensing something was amiss, Bogie came to the door and surveyed the scene in silence.

"We won't tell the madam about this," he said, quietly, and with that he flicked off the light, closed the door, and went to the bar for a drink. Later, when Betty was occupied elsewhere, he and his assistant rewound the film.

FOR AN UNLIKELY COUPLE of friends, you would have to go a long way
before you found a more oddly matched pair than Bogart and "Prince"
Michael Romanoff. Bogart with his proper upbringing, his casual manner of
dress, his raffish sense of humor, and his occasional tough manner, contrasted
sharply with Romanoff, illegal immigrant who had lived for many years
one jump ahead of the police (and sometimes one jump behind), a man of
impeccable manners and a carefully cultivated Oxford accent, and a man so
persnickety about his appearance that he wore his jacket at all times, even in
the barber's chair. (He was so small that two people could lift him easily and
toss him about like a beanbag, but no matter how hard they tried they could
seldom separate him from his jacket.)

Romanoff was born on February 21, 1886, in Vilna, Lithuania, then as now
a part of Russia. His surname was Geguzonoff, the anglicization of which
probably led American reporters to dub him Gerguson, and he adopted the
name Romanoff at first tentatively and then, when he found that certain
segments of Long Island society were impressed by it, he put it to full use and
got as much mileage out of it as he could. He was an international traveler,
always without a passport and often in jail, but he had a manner about him
and a quickness of wit that laughed at iron bars, and he was never detained
for very long. His transatlantic sailings were likely to be under the tarpaulin
of a lifeboat, from which he would emerge once at sea and, looking miracul-
ously well tailored, strike up an acquaintance with someone whose cabin he

could share. His debarkation, a sticky matter for those without papers, was accomplished by donning a porter's apron, carrying a few loads of luggage, and then doffing the apron and leaving the pier. Always immaculate and always self-possessed, he moved in a faintly regal way wherever he went.

He and Bogart met, probably in the early 1930s, at a Sunday *soiree* at the home of the Agronsky sisters, in Greenwich Village. (Lee Agronsky, who had known Bogart since about 1919, subsequently married Ira Gershwin.) Their friendship was not a close one at the time since their paths didn't often converge, with Bogart in the theater and Romanoff picking his way wherever he could best make out — although he did have a brief fling at the theater, when he did a bit as "himself" in Cole Porter's *Jubilee* in 1935. In 1937 he transferred his base of operations to Hollywood, and there he found himself in a group that consisted of, among other people, Mark Hellinger, Robert Benchley, Charles Butterworth, Roland Young, John McClain, and, naturally, Bogart.

In 1939, wearying of the peripatetic life, he decided to settle down and start a business of his own, and he approached his friends with the proposition that they buy stock in a bar he intended to set up on North Rodeo Drive, in Beverly Hills. Several of them bought stock, at fifteen hundred dollars a share, and they were appalled when they found out that he wanted to make it into a restaurant as well. Have sandwiches or a free lunch, they told him, but for God's sake don't get into the restaurant business. Undeterred, he went ahead and turned it into the most popular and successful restaurant in Hollywood, on a par with if not surpassing the legendary Chasen's. So successful was it, in fact, that some local gangsters decided to see if they could get in on the action, and to forestall any such move the original stockholders turned their certificates back to Romanoff, so that he could have full ownership.

Bogart, as one of the originals, was a constant patron of the restaurant, both in its first location and later, after 1951, when it moved to larger and more ornate quarters on South Rodeo. He had his own table, next to the entrance, and he came there for lunch virtually every day when he wasn't working, and

A chess game with Mike Romanoff, who seems confident about the outcome. The third man is actor Robert Coote, soon to go back to Broadway and appear in what he described as "some musical version of *Pygmalion*."

The Bogarts with Mike Romanoff, whom Bogie sometimes addressed as "King."

two or three times a week for dinner. He liked to dress informally at lunch, and this led him into a head-on collision with Romanoff, who insisted that all his customers wear ties. Once, when Bogart came in unshaven and wearing a sports shirt, Romanoff said, "Bogart, you're lowering the tone of my joint when you come in looking like that."

"Then I'll take my business to the Brown Derby," Bogart replied.

"Why inflict yourself on them?" said Romanoff. He gave Bogart a tie, which Bogart immediately put in his pocket, claiming it was just a decoration, and with that tied a napkin around his neck.

The next time Bogart came in he seemed at first to be wearing no necktie, but when Romanoff got closer he saw he was wearing a one-inch-wide, enameled bow tie, which he'd had a jeweler make and put on a pin. Romanoff examined it with a glass, and finally said, "Damn you — I hate you, but it passes."

They had a running chess contest; Romanoff had studied under a master, and was one of the few people who could beat Bogart at the game. (Art Buchwald was another.) They played chess by mail, by telephone, and in person, and there were times when Bogart would wait around the restaurant until all the luncheon trade had left, and then he and the proprietor would sit in a corner and play chess while the waiters cleared off the tables and reset them for dinner. The difference in their games could be gauged by the fact that their rules stipulated they would play twenty games in a row, and if Romanoff lost one he had to pay a hundred dollars. Conversely, if Bogart didn't win one in twenty, he had to pay the hundred. It was usually Bogart who did the paying, but once, to his great delight, he took the fourteenth game in a series, and when Romanoff gave him the money he gloated briefly and then sent it to a friend in the hospital. Probably his greatest coup, however, was when he and Richard Brooks set up a telephone game with Romanoff and enlisted the aid of a man named Steiner, then a United States chess champion, to take the other end of the phone. They didn't tell Romanoff whom he was playing; they simply phoned in his moves and relayed the replies. Romanoff started out full of confidence as always, but after about a dozen moves he realized

Carrying Mrs. Billy Wilder at a party at
the Danny Kayes' in August of 1954.
Richard Rodgers is politely amused.

Another view of the same action. Mrs.
Wilder's reaction is unrecorded.

he was up against a master, and after twenty moves he resigned. Bogart's glee was as great as if he had actually done the winning.

Another of his practical jokes on Romanoff backfired. It was at a Sunday croquet game, which in Hollywood is played with all the seriousness and concentration of open-heart surgery, and Romanoff had just put his ball through a wicket and was lining up the next shot when, very quietly, Bogart said, "You didn't go through that wicket."

Romanoff looked at him in amazement, and said, "I certainly did."

He returned his attention to the ball, and was about to hit it when Bogart said, "You can say what you like, your ball went around the wicket, not through it."

This kept up until, finally, Romanoff exploded. Usually a man of icy dignity, he flew into a shouting tantrum, and wound up by denouncing Bogart and all his forebears, and banning him from the restaurant. The exact phraseology of his proscription was, "And you can't come in my joint any more!"

A few days later Bogart went around to the restaurant, opened the door a crack, and threw his hat inside. After a proper pause he followed it in, and in the fullness of time and several drinks the incident was buried.

Anent Bogart's various capers, Romanoff once described him as "a first-class person with an obsessive compulsion to behave like a second-class person." He knew Bogart was basically a gentleman, but thought that for some reason he was afraid to show it. Furthermore, he had the feeling that Bogart was being protective about him; he didn't know why, and it made him uneasy.

In the early 1950s, King Paul and Queen Frederica of Greece made a visit to Hollywood as guests of Mr. and Mrs. Spyros Skouras. They stayed at the Beverly Wilshire Hotel, and one day while walking with his equerry the king noticed Romanoff's, with its reversed Rs on the door, and he went inside. It developed that John, the bartender, was Greek; the king took to making his visit a daily affair, and in short order met Bogart, who among other things taught him the value of Fernet Branca bitters as a hangover remedy. Bogart used on occasion to call Romanoff "King," and he now, as a needle to Romanoff because it was rotten protocol, took to calling King Paul "King," as in "Good morning, King"; "This round is on me, King"; and so on. The king was mildly amused, but Romanoff, as Bogart had intended, was as irritated as a parent whose child has belched in front of company.

This friendship with the king paid off, for Romanoff, in an extraordinary way. On June 27, 1958, following an Act of Congress to make him eligible,* he received his United States citizenship papers. He and his wife, Gloria, whom he had married in 1948, went down to the Federal Building in Los Angeles, and prior to the naturalization ceremony the clerk asked if there was anyone present who had a foreign title to renounce before becoming a citizen. Gloria, who was sitting in the back of the room, saw her husband's ears turn red, then grow even redder when the clerk repeated the question. Finally, the clerk came to Romanoff and put it to him directly. Flustered and embarrassed, Romanoff renounced his nonexistent title of prince, and thereafter became a citizen. As he and Gloria made for the Passport Office he said, "Wouldn't you know — on the very last day, I find a true believer!"

He also found that, as a citizen and celebrity, life was different from what it had been in the old days. J. Edgar Hoover offered all possible cooperation in making Romanoff's first legal trip abroad a pleasant one, and although Romanoff didn't ask for it there was an FBI man waiting for them in a car when they arrived at Orly Airport in Paris. The agent drove them to the Ritz, where a red carpet was being unrolled, and while Gloria was incredulous the ex-prince took it all in his stride. He was never more regal as he alit from the car and started up the carpet; it then developed that the carpet was for the king of Greece, who was just leaving the hotel, and Gloria cowered behind in the car, expecting her husband to be once again

---

* House of Representatives Bill #8348, from Eastland, Committee on the Judiciary, for the relief of Michael Romanoff, the purpose to grant status of permanent residence in the U.S. to Michael Romanoff as of December 22, 1932. Sponsors included John Kennedy, Richard Nixon, Jacob Javits.

208

At a Valentine party at Romanoff's, February 11, 1956. It was the last big party the Bogarts attended. Other celebrants are Phyllis Kirk and Adolph Green.

The Bogarts and the Coopers share a joke. Comparing this picture with the following one, it would appear that Betty's dental work compares favorably with her husband's. This book may be unique, in that it shows ondo-oral exposures of both the principal characters.

The Bogarts at a party at the home of Mr. and Mrs. Charles Lederer on New Year's Eve, 1955. If this looks like the dress Betty wore on another occasion, it is. And why not?

New Year's Eve, 1954, *chez* Lederer. The Lederers' New Year's parties were as regular and as well attended as the Academy Award evenings.

Welcoming the New Year.

whisked off to pokey. But the king recognized him and greeted him warmly, and they exchanged cigarettes and lights and reminisced about their times with Bogart, and the king thanked Romanoff for all he'd done for him in Hollywood. It was an encounter that one of the real Romanoffs might well have envied.

Gloria and Michael Romanoff were also in on the establishment of the Holmby Hills Rat Pack, a loosely knit organization that was born in the spring of 1955, when Nöel Coward was making a personal appearance at the Desert Inn, in Las Vegas. Sinatra, always a big man for group action, organized an expedition to attend Coward's opening night, and to that end he chartered a bus, which took the pilgrims from the Bogarts' house to the airport, where they boarded a chartered airplane for the trip to Las Vegas. The group included the Bogarts, the Romanoffs, David and Hjördis Niven, Irving "Swifty" Lazar and Martha Hyer, Jimmie Van Heusen and Angie Dickinson, Charles Feldman and Capucine, Mr. and Mrs. George Axelrod, Mr. and Mrs. Charles Lederer, and Judy Garland and Sid Luft; there were different colored armbands for different occasions (cocktails, lunch, dinner, etc.), and everyone was required to wear an armband and move with the rest of the group. In the Sands Hotel they had adjoining rooms, to which Sinatra had a master key so as to be able to rout out any potential shirkers, and on one morning there was a simple order to Room Service for three hundred Bloody Marys, which kept relays of waiters shuttling back and forth like the Berlin airlift. By some miracle they managed to see Coward's opening, and then they spent the next four days gambling and gamboling, finally resorting to pills to keep themselves going. (Sinatra was the only one who seemed untouched by the carousing, and wound up as fresh as he had started.) Finally, on the fourth day, Betty surveyed the wreckage of the party and said, "You look like a goddamn rat pack," and with that the group became official. Sinatra was named Pack Leader, Betty was Den Mother, Bogie was Director of Public Relations, and Sid Luft was Acting Cage Master. The present reporter, although not one of the originals, was later named Honorary Recording Secretary, but since there was little to record the post was a hollow one. It consisted mainly of designing a Pack coat of arms, with Bogie's motto: "Never rat on a rat."

216

In the course of time the Pack deteriorated into the Clan, with a new set of members and a new set of ideals, and finally, it went the way of all noble experiments. Without Bogart, it didn't seem to make much sense.

I<small>N</small> 1953, Bogart bought the rights to James Helvick's crime novel *Beat the Devil*. He thought it might be made into another *Maltese Falcon,* and to this end he got Huston, with whom he had had such spectacular success, to direct the picture, and a brace of expert writers, Peter Viertel and Anthony Veiller, to do the screenplay. Santana shared the production credit with Romulus Films, and Bogart was an unlisted producer, with what finally turned out to be more than a half-million dollars of his own money in the venture. The cast, aside from the star, included Jennifer Jones, Gina Lollobrigida, Robert Morley, and Peter Lorre, the last of whom had been in four previous films with Bogart, including *Maltese Falcon* and *Casablanca,* and had almost reached the status of a good-luck token.

The first problem was that the script didn't work. Bogart's succinct analysis of it was that "it stinks," and he began to think perhaps the whole project should be shelved. But the company was already assembled in Ravello, the small Italian town on the Adriatic where most of the action would be shot, and Huston convinced him that all was not lost. Viertel and Veiller departed and Huston took over the script, and after a week or so of tinkering he had a brainstorm and invited Truman Capote to come to Ravello and be the screenwriter. Capote came, and what had been a fairly straight, if complicated, adventure story turned gradually, through Capote's pixie sense of humor, into a lighthearted parody. However, not all the actors understood this, and progress was painfully slow. They were two weeks

218

behind schedule when they started shooting, and they got progressively farther behind with every day that passed. In the end, the shooting consumed three and a half months, or two months longer than had been intended.

All events, both large and small, seemed to conspire to delay. The weather in Ravello was bright and beautiful in the morning, but invariably around noon the skies became overcast, so it was impossible to match a morning shot with anything done in the afternoon. And Miss Lollobrigida insisted on doing her own makeup, so no shot in which she appeared could get under way much before 11 A.M. Also, there were three crews; one Italian crew, which happened to be made up mostly of Communists, was the best, but since this was during the McCarthy period they had to have another, non-Communist, crew, who turned out to be totally inept. A third, English, crew was all right, but obviously couldn't be used too much in preference to the locals. Unnecessary towers and ramps and scaffolds were built, to keep the nonworking crews busy.

Then there were the imponderable, or act of God, delays. In Rome, Huston had seen a man he thought would be perfect as the purser of the ship (in the story, the actors are stranded in Italy by a mechanical breakdown on their ship), so he approached him and asked if he spoke English. The man, whose name was Mario Perroni, said, "Yes," and was thereupon hired, without revealing that he had just exhausted his vocabulary of the language. This didn't become apparent until the shooting of his one big scene, in which he had to say to Bogart: "Mr. Dannreuther, the captain of the S.S. *Nyanga* presents his compliments, and wishes to advise you that owing to the failure of the oil pump, the sailing of the S.S. *Nyanga* has been postponed." According to eyewitness accounts Huston's face, when Perroni struggled with this mouthful, was a study. The line was tried over and over again with no better success; Huston led him through it like a choirmaster but to no avail, and finally, more or less as a way of changing the subject, Huston became interested in Perroni's hairdo, and spent the rest of the morning combing and recombing the would-be actor's hair. His lines were eventually dubbed in by Peter Ustinov.

It wasn't only the Italians who had trouble with their lines. Miss Jones played the part of a compulsive liar, and for some reason had difficulty in one scene with the proper shading of the word "No." Huston, dressed in riding clothes and wearing a brown cap with uptied earflaps and a tinted windshield hung from the visor, sat with her under a beach umbrella and rehearsed her in saying "No" the way he wanted it, and she, wearing a blond wig and furiously stitching on a piece of needlepoint, kept saying "No" back to him the way he didn't want it. And Peter Lorre had his own ideas about how he should behave, which didn't always coincide with those of the director. Naturally, such things used up time.

Through all this Bogart drifted like a brooding moose, sometimes with his hairpiece and sometimes without, while the townspeople watched from behind rope barriers, and Capote kept darting down with the latest addition to the script, then returning to his hotel to write the next day's shooting. Thirty children, retained from a local orphanage for one scene, waited with remarkable restraint behind the ropes for two weeks until their shot was made, and very often all they watched was the inch-by-inch changing of the camera track to get an angle that satisfied Huston. Bogart could almost literally see his money flowing through the town gutters, and his only solace was his nightly call to Betty, back in California.

When, finally, the picture was released, the reaction was divided. Some reviewers thought it a disaster and some thought it brilliant satire; the *Times* was one of the latter, and Otis Guernsey, in the *Herald Tribune*, called it "a burlesque of all movie melodramas," adding that "the workmanship is marvelous to behold, but there is no design." (Little did he know.) Bogart, he thought, was "a straight man, used by Huston to set off chain reactions among the comedians." Harry Kurnitz, the celebrated wit and writer, remarked that no matter where you came in during the running of the picture, you seemed to have missed at least half. When, a while later, the Bogarts were leaving the United States to go to Europe, a Customs official said to Bogart, "If you make one more movie like *Beat the Devil*, we won't let you back." "I won't want to come back," Bogart replied, thereby giving his opinion of the picture. He thought it had been ruined, and that only the phony intellectuals thought it was funny. Originally it lost money, but slowly over the years a cult began to form around it, and by now it has made back more than its original investment.

✠

His next seven pictures were a mixed bag, distinguished primarily for the variety of roles he played. It was almost as though he were touching all bases, playing every conceivable kind of character just to show he could do it. By all odds the most successful was that of Captain Queeg in *The Caine Mutiny*, which he did immediately following *Beat the Devil*. Having had enough of being his own producer he was glad to sign in a Stanley Kramer Company production, which was directed by Edward Dmytryk and released through Columbia. Furthermore, the part was one he could, as the actors say, get his teeth into.

Not that Captain Queeg is a simple character; far from it. The iron-fisted disciplinarian, who lapses into disorientation when things go wrong, is familiar enough as an idea (and there were plenty of them in the armed forces; one is tempted to believe that Herman Wouk, who wrote the novel, must have sailed with one L. C. Quiggle, a destroyer skipper in the early days of the war), but for an actor to make the transition convincing requires finesse of the highest order. This Bogart managed to do; Otis Guernsey wrote of "a strong performance by Humphrey Bogart in shifty, neurotic closeups, climaxed when his face falls apart in slack surrender during his collapse on the witness stand." Bosley Crowther thought that "Humphrey Bogart's twitchy performance of the 'by-the-book' Captain Queeg is a bit in the usual Bogart manner [? — Ed], but, by and large, it is sound." He concluded that *The Caine Mutiny,* "though somewhat garbled, is a vibrant film."

For his performance Bogart received his third Academy Award nomination, but Marlon Brando had revenge and got the Oscar for *On the Waterfront.*

Sabrina, Bogart's next picture in 1954, had him cast as a slightly stuffy older brother to William Holden, a playboy in love with Audrey Hepburn, the daughter of the family chauffeur. The story was taken from the play *Sabrina Fair,* by Samuel Taylor; it was directed by Billy Wilder, and the screenplay, by Wilder, Taylor, and Ernest Lehman, had been written with Cary Grant in mind for the older brother. At the last minute, however, Grant changed his mind (he also backed away from *A Star Is Born,* thereby missing the two big hits of 1954), and the part was rewritten for Bogart. His friction with Holden has already been chronicled; there was also little love lost between him and Miss Hepburn, and it was a tribute to the professionalism of all concerned that the picture ever made it into the can and became the success it was. There was, incidentally, one scene of a fight between Bogart and Holden — a bang-up, wild-swinging, movie-type fight — and, for reasons that nobody is prepared to explain, *Life* magazine had a still photographer up in the flies, filming the sequence. If they had heard of the undercurrent of friction running through the company (and it was certainly no secret) they could have been hoping that one of the actors might cut loose with a real punch and trigger a fight of historic proportions; however, at this remove it is impossible to nail anything down. People connected with the picture get a blank expression when the idea is mentioned, and then they discuss something else.

The Barefoot Contessa, the last of the four Bogart pictures released in 1954, was less successful. Written and directed by Joseph L. Mankiewicz, and released through United Artists, it had Bogart as a washed-up movie director, trying to make a comeback by doing a picture for a superglamorous newcomer. The whole thing was told in flashbacks, starting at the glamorous newcomer's rain-soaked grave, and the story became so long and involved that audience attention began to wander, and a certain indifference set in. As Guernsey summed it up: "This movie has style in places and a certain flamboyance, but the level of its human drama is routine." But it did have Ava Gardner as the newcomer, and Edmund O'Brien won an Academy Award for his portrayal of a bombastic press agent, and that, added to Bogart's usual professional performance, gave it a fair amount on the plus side. It was not a unique role for Bogart; he'd done the same sort of thing almost twenty years before, in *Stand-In,* but it was at least different from the others in his final period.

Then, for a really sharp change of pace, he did the comedy *We're No Angels,* adapted from the stage play *My Three Angels* (in turn adapted from the French play *La Cuisine des Anges,* by Albert Husson), which involved three escapees from Devil's Island. Aldo Ray and Peter Ustinov were his coescapees; the director was Michael Curtiz of *Casablanca* fame, and the only trouble was that the story was of such a wispy, farcical nature that what had worked well in the intimacy of the stage came through a little flat-footed in the grandeur of Paramount VistaVision. It was like a rendition of "Nola" by the American Legion Drum & Bugle Corps. The change of title from the stage to the movie version brings out a curious phenomenon that haunted Bogart throughout his career: no matter what part he was playing, if there was no title that sprang readily to mind the producers opted for something that had a sinister ring to it, echoing all the gangster films. *They Drive by Night,* for instance, sounded a more ominous note than *Romance on the Road,* which the picture could just as easily have been titled; *The Wagons Roll at Night* might as well have been *Son of Kid Galahad* or *Don't Play with Crazy Lions;* and *All Through the Night* is less provocative but more sinister than *Who Killed the Cheesecake Baker?,* which is what the story was all about. The prize for idiotic titling, however, goes to *Deadline — U.S.A.,* written and directed by Richard Brooks in 1950, which was a story about a crusading newspaperman and the title of which means absolutely nothing. Date*line — U.S.A.* would have made some sense, but the word "dead" had to be brought in to give it that sinister ring, and sense be damned.

Having played practically everything else, Bogart next took a fling at being a priest — or, rather, a downed American airman in China posing as a priest. The picture was *The Left Hand of God,* adapted by Alfred Hayes from the novel by William E. Barrett, and it was directed by his old friend Edward Dmytryk and shot in CinemaScope. (This was during the period when the movies, terrified by the burgeoning growth of television, were trying everything they could think of, from three-dimensional pictures —

which often induced nausea — to screens so wide they practically wrapped themselves around the audience, in order to win back the viewing public. What they often as not forgot was that a good story needs no gimmicks.) In the case of *The Left Hand of God,* the director and the screenwriter took the critical rap for not realizing the story's potential. At the premiere of the film, Bogart was collared in the lobby by an interviewer with a microphone, who asked him if this was his favorite role.

"No," he replied. "I wouldn't say that."

"How does it feel to be a priest?" the man persisted.

"How would *I* know?" said Bogart, thereby ending the interview.

Then, almost like an alcoholic grabbing a bottle after a long stretch on the wagon, Bogart went back to the Duke Mantee character. In *The Desperate Hours,* written by Joseph Hayes and based on his novel and play, he turned in a performance that showed he had lost none of his touch for that kind of part; in fact, with his growth as an actor he gave it a new force and dimension. Fredric March played the father in a household taken over by three escaped convicts, and under William Wyler's direction every potential of the story was realized to the fullest. The one flaw — a nagging implausibility in one sequence — kept the picture from being a complete artistic success, but Bogart's performance was such that only the most carping of critics would care too much. Crowther wrote that it was "a crafty and cracking screen thriller . . . brilliantly presented [but] it just doesn't make too good sense." He called Bogart "a fearful symbol of brute force, impervious to pity or regard for the rights of other men," and went on, "Not since Mr. Bogart's appearance in 'The Petrified Forest' has he shown quite the smirking, squint-eyed cunning and sub surface ferocity he spreads upon the screen."

And then came *The Harder They Fall,* a prizefight picture in which he was an ex–sports columnist hired to publicize an Argentine man-mountain of little talent. The picture, written by Philip Yordan from the novel by Budd

Schulberg, was directed by Mark Robson for Columbia, and was an indictment of the gangster elements in the boxing business. In the end Bogart, sickened by the criminal brutality and dishonesty he has seen, vows to write a series of pieces that will get boxing banned in the United States — a somewhat naïve thought from so apparently sophisticated a character.

The next picture on his schedule was one he and Betty were going to do together: *Melville Goodwin, U.S.A.*, from J. P. Marquand's novel of the same name (the U.S.A. stood for United States Army). It was the story of a hard-bitten general and his affair with a lady of some status as a celebrity — like Claire Booth Luce, Carmel Snow, and Eleanor Roosevelt, all rolled into one — and it had a certain timeliness in that a general was then President of the United States. Milton Sperling, a Warner son-in-law, was the producer (he had his own company, United States Pictures, which used the Warner lot) and H. C. Potter was signed as director. The matter of writing the script was a long and complicated one — Sperling thought so highly of Ring Lardner, Jr.'s *Woman of the Year* that he had it run and rerun for his own writers, to give them a hint — and by the time the screenplay, by Roland Kibbee, was finally ready for production, Bogart was on his way to the hospital. The picture was finally made, starring Kirk Douglas and Susan Hayward, and titled *Top Secret Affair*.

In a corner at a party.

IT STARTED with a small, dry cough. He would cough, then as a reflex touch his breastbone, as though to locate the source of the twinge. The doctor's first theory was that it was an acid condition; perhaps he should try omitting the breakfast orange juice, and see if that helped. He did, but the cough and the twinge persisted. Then medication was tried, but it did no good and he gave it up, and other medication was tried and he gave that up, too. He still kept coughing, and touching his breastbone.

Then one day near the end of February (this was 1956) he and Betty were at Romanoff's for lunch, and when you looked at her it was obvious something was wrong. He was bright and cheerful and chatty, but she looked as though she'd just been kicked by a horse. To people who stopped by their table, he said he'd opened up a whole new field of medicine; if he'd taken his prescriptions as ordered, he'd have covered up the fact that he had a growth that needed removing (a biopsy, done in the doctor's office, had revealed this), and now, by not taking his medicine, he'd forced the condition into the open where something could be done about it. All very funny, except for the look on Betty's face. But he kept up the act, giving the old gung-ho sign when anyone asked how he was feeling.

As he and Betty drove to Good Samaritan Hospital, he dropped the act long enough to say, "I've never been sick in my life, and now I'll probably spend the rest of my life with doctors."

The operation was brutal. They went in from his back, opening him like a side of beef, and cut away his esophagus, around which the cancer had wrapped itself. It took nine hours, and during that time Swifty Lazar looked after Betty and tried to keep her mind busy. For Lazar this was a sacrifice of heroic proportions, because his fear and loathing of hospitals bordered on the psychotic, and for him even to walk in the door of one was akin to another man's putting his hand in a fire.

When he was strong enough to be moved, Bogie was brought home in an ambulance, and as he was wheeled up to the front door on a stretcher Betty was there to greet him. When he saw her his eyes puddled over, and he said, "People say why do you get married, and look what I've got here."

For nine months and more, following the operation, he tried to believe he'd recover. He knew from the first he'd had cancer, and he felt this was nothing to be ashamed of or to be whispered about, but following the operation he felt that all he had to do was put on a little weight, and he'd be all right. Or if only he could get back to work, then he'd feel better. But the cancer kept gnawing away at his already emaciated frame, and the most he could do was come down and sit in the library for a little while at six o'clock each afternoon, and have a couple of drinks with selected friends who dropped around. Spencer Tracy, Katharine Hepburn, the Nivens, Huston, Lazar, Nunnally Johnson (who came back from Georgia when he heard of Bogie's condition), Sinatra, Harry Kurnitz, and a few others were allowed in, singly or in pairs, to have a drink and try to pretend that everything was going to be fine. He kept smoking because, as he pointed out sourly, your esophagus has nothing to do with your lungs, and he kept drinking, either Scotch or martinis, because he liked to, and he was not about to change the habits of a lifetime just because he was a little underweight. Betty is firm in her conviction that nobody ever heard him say anything to indicate he knew he was dying; anyone who says that, she maintains, is simply not telling

John Huston following Betty and Steve into the car.

the truth. So the testimony of people like Natalie Schafer and Gloria Romanoff, to whom, when Betty was out of the room, he said how wonderful she'd been for him, must be interpreted as a statement of that fact and nothing else, with no premonitions of the future implied or to be inferred. During the last couple of months he didn't want the children to see him — presumably, they'd be allowed to after he'd put on some weight, and was once again his old self.

When the stairs became too much, a service elevator — dumbwaiter, really — had the trays and shelves taken out so that his wheelchair could be accommodated, and this way he made the trip down and up each afternoon. Then, finally, that had to be discontinued, and one at a time certain friends were allowed upstairs. Raymond Massey was one of those who came to see him, and the last day he was there Bogie asked him to tell an old dialect story, about a Baptist minister in Georgia, which he'd always found funny and which Massey told at great length and with much elaboration. Knowing that it would hurt Bogie to laugh (everything hurt by then), Massey looked at Betty for advice.

"Go ahead," she told him. "He'd rather laugh and hurt, than not laugh at all."

So Massey told the story, and Bogie laughed, and hurt, and Massey said good-bye and left.

Sunday, January 13, 1957, was much like every Sunday in the recent past — a period that seemed to have been going on forever. By now the whole thing was a way of life; there was no immediate thought of Bogie's dying, but there was also no thought of his getting better. Time seemed to have stopped at a particularly hideous period, and people went mechanically through the motions of everyday living. Betty went down and got the Sunday paper, and when she brought it upstairs Bogie was half propped up in bed, shaving. She said she was going out to get the kids from Sunday school, and he said OK, and when she got back he had drifted into a coma. He remained that way until 2:10 the following morning, when he was pronounced officially dead. Betty took a short while to pull herself together, then started calling those who should be told. It was 4 A.M. when she got the Nivens, and in a very low voice said, "My darling husband is gone."

⌘

He had a theory that "life is for the living"; he felt that any grieving or mourning was a disservice to the departed, and that the only thing to do was have a drink, and carry on from there. (He believed that no matter what happened, the world was always two drinks below normal.) He remembered how Mrs. Will Rogers, on being told of her husband's death in an airplane crash, had doubled over as though hit in the stomach, then slowly straightened up and gone on with what she'd been saying. That, he felt, was the way people should behave. That showed true class.

Which brings us back to that word again. He achieved class through his integrity and his devotion to what he thought was right, and if there were those who either didn't agree or who saw it in another light, that was their business. He believed in being direct, simple, and honest, all on his own terms, and this ruffled some people and endeared him to others. He couldn't have cared less.

In the interest of simplicity, Betty kept the formal trappings to a minimum. On Thursday, January 17, a brief service was held in All Saints' Episcopal Church, in Beverly Hills; a glass-enclosed model of *Santana* was where the coffin would normally be, and the Reverend Kermit Castellanos read the Ten Commandments and Tennyson's "Crossing the Bar." John Huston delivered a brief, eloquent eulogy, then Betty asked people back to the house for a drink. While this was going on Bogart was being cremated at Forest Lawn, and the gold whistle from *To Have and Have Not* was with him.

DRAWING BY WM. HAMILTON, © 1973 THE NEW YORKER MAGAZINE, INC.

"I like it. It's Humphrey Bogart without the arrogance."

Acknowledgments

A NUMBER OF PEOPLE CONTRIBUTED, in a greater or lesser degree, to the making of this book. Foremost among them, both alphabetically and in the author's gratitude, is Lauren Bacall, whose wholehearted cooperation went a long way toward making the whole thing possible. The others include Ingrid Bergman, Art Buchwald, Sammy Cahn, Mrs. Gertrude Chase, Mrs. Dave Chasen, Betty Comden, Alistair Cooke, John Cromwell, John Crosby, Betty Furness, Tay Garnett, Mrs. Ira Gershwin, Adolph Green, Mrs. Eric Hatch, William Holden, Sam Jaffe, Nunnally Johnson, Charles Lederer, Commander Joseph C. Lewis, Jr., USN, Cynthia Lindsay, Mrs. Kenneth MacKenna, Raymond Massey, Jo Mielziner, Mrs. Mary Baker Miller, David Niven, Edith Oliver, George Oppenheimer, Allen Rivkin, Mrs. Michael Romanoff, Stuart Rose, Mr. and Mrs. John Barry Ryan III, Natalie Schafer, Frank Sinatra, Arthur Sircom, Mrs. Franklin B. Tuttle, Peter Viertel, Mrs. Diana Vreeland, Robert Wallsten, Richard Watts, Jr., Hobart G. Weekes, Mrs. Louise Dahl Wolfe, and Collier Young.

Also, Georgiana Francisco of IFA, Roberts Jackson of Culver Pictures, Leonard Miall of the BBC, the staff of the Theatre Collection at the Museum of the Performing Arts, Elaine Richard of Little, Brown and Company, and Marie Schuman, Caroline Turman and Susan Kismaric of the Time-Life Picture Collection.

And a special genuflection to Marjorie Benchley and the *fils cadet*, N. R. Benchley, for assorted assists, errands, and chores.

Motion Pictures in Which
Humphrey Bogart Appeared

1930	*Broadway's Like That*	Vitaphone Corporation–Warner Brothers
1930	*A Devil with Women*	Fox
1930	*Up the River*	Fox
1931	*Body and Soul*	Fox
1931	*Bad Sister*	Universal
1931	*Women of All Nations*	Fox
1931	*A Holy Terror*	Fox
1932	*Love Affair*	Columbia
1932	*Big City Blues*	Warner Brothers
1932	*Three on a Match*	First National–Warner Brothers
1934	*Midnight*	All-Star Productions–First National
1936	*The Petrified Forest*	Warner Brothers
1936	*Bullets or Ballots*	First National–Warner Brothers
1936	*Two Against the World*	First National–Warner Brothers
1936	*China Clipper*	First National–Warner Brothers
1936	*Isle of Fury*	Warner Brothers
1937	*Black Legion*	Warner Brothers
1937	*The Great O'Malley*	Warner Brothers
1937	*Marked Woman*	First National–Warner Brothers
1937	*Kid Galahad*	Warner Brothers
1937	*San Quentin*	First National–Warner Brothers
1937	*Dead End*	Samuel Goldwyn–United Artists
1937	*Stand-In*	Walter Wanger–United Artists

1938	*Swing Your Lady*	Warner Brothers
1938	*Crime School*	First National–Warner Brothers
1938	*Men Are Such Fools*	Warner Brothers
1938	*The Amazing Dr. Clitterhouse*	First National–Warner Brothers
1938	*Racket Busters*	Warner Brothers
1938	*Angels with Dirty Faces*	First National–Warner Brothers
1939	*King of the Underworld*	Warner Brothers
1939	*The Oklahoma Kid*	Warner Brothers
1939	*Dark Victory*	First National–Warner Brothers
1939	*You Can't Get Away with Murder*	First National–Warner Brothers
1939	*The Roaring Twenties*	Warner Brothers–First National
1939	*The Return of Dr. X*	Warner Brothers–First National
1939	*Invisible Stripes*	Warner Brothers–First National
1940	*Virginia City*	Warner Brothers–First National
1940	*It All Came True*	Warner Brothers–First National
1940	*Brother Orchid*	Warner Brothers–First National
1940	*They Drive by Night*	Warner Brothers–First National
1941	*High Sierra*	Warner Brothers–First National
1941	*The Wagons Roll at Night*	Warner Brothers–First National
1941	*The Maltese Falcon*	Warner Brothers–First National
1942	*All Through the Night*	Warner Brothers–First National
1942	*The Big Shot*	Warner Brothers–First National
1942	*Across the Pacific*	Warner Brothers–First National
1943	*Casablanca*	Warner Brothers–First National
1943	*Action in the North Atlantic*	Warner Brothers–First National
1943	*Thank Your Lucky Stars*	Warner Brothers–First National
1943	*Sahara*	Columbia
1944	*Passage to Marseilles*	Warner Brothers–First National
1944	*Report from the Front*	Red Cross–National Screen Service
1945	*To Have and Have Not*	Warner Brothers–First National
1945	*Conflict*	Warner Brothers–First National
1945	*Hollywood Victory Caravan*	Treasury Department–Paramount Pictures
1946	*Two Guys from Milwaukee*	Warner Brothers–First National

1946	*The Big Sleep*	Warner Brothers–First National
1947	*Dead Reckoning*	Columbia
1947	*The Two Mrs. Carrolls*	Warner Brothers–First National
1947	*Dark Passage*	Warner Brothers–First National
1948	*Always Together*	Warner Brothers–First National
1948	*The Treasure of the Sierra Madre*	Warner Brothers–First National
1948	*Key Largo*	Warner Brothers–First National
1949	*Knock on Any Door*	Santana Productions–Columbia
1949	*Tokyo Joe*	Santana Productions–Columbia
1950	*Chain Lightning*	Warner Brothers–First National
1950	*In a Lonely Place*	Santana Productions–Columbia
1950	*Deadline — U.S.A.*	Twentieth Century–Fox
1951	*The Enforcer*	United States Picture–Warner Brothers
1951	*Sirocco*	Santana Productions–Columbia
1951	*The African Queen*	Horizon-Romulus Productions–United Artists
1952	U.S. Savings Bonds short	Metro-Goldwyn-Mayer
1953	*Battle Circus*	Metro-Goldwyn-Mayer
1954	*Beat the Devil*	Santana-Romulus Productions–United Artists
1954	*The Caine Mutiny*	Stanley Kramer Productions–Columbia
1954	*Sabrina*	Paramount
1954	*The Barefoot Contessa*	Figaro Inc. Productions–United Artists
1955	*We're No Angels*	Paramount
1955	*The Left Hand of God*	Twentieth Century–Fox
1955	*The Desperate Hours*	Paramount
1956	*The Harder They Fall*	Columbia

Picture Credits

Karsh, Ottawa: frontispiece

Courtesy of Lauren Bacall: 8, 18, 124, 168 *(top)*

Courtesy of United Artists Television, Inc.: 9, 10, 14–15, 41, 43 *(top)*

Courtesy of Arthur Sircom: 13

Culver Pictures: 23 *(both)*, 24, 26, 28 *(both)*, 29, 33, 34–35, 36, 42, 48, 60–61, 62–63, 73, 76–77, 85, 91, 92 *(both)*, 93, 94 *(both)*, 99, 102–103, 106–107, 108, 109, 110, 118, 120 *(both)*, 121, 122 *(both)*, 130–131, 132–133, 179, 180, 191, 192

Courtesy of Stuart Rose: 31

Time-Life Picture Agency, © Time Inc.: 43 *(bottom)*

Drawing by Frueh, Copyright 1935, 1963 The New Yorker Magazine, Inc.: 58

United Press International: 70, 165, 195, 198

Courtesy of Mr. and Mrs. Raymond Massey: 74

Photograph by Ralph Warren, courtesy of Gertrude Chase: 83

Courtesy of Mrs. Eric Hatch: 96–97 *(all)*

Photograph by Gjon Mili: 116–117

Photograph by Louise Dahl-Wolfe: 125, 126 *(both)*, 127, 128 *(both)*

Pix Inc.: 134

Courtesy of Mary Baker Miller: 141

Martha Holmes, *Life*, © 1972 Time Inc.: 161

Courtesy of Maude Chasen: 162–163

Photograph by Murray Garrett, Graphic House: 168 *(bottom)*

Courtesy of Gertrude Chase: 171, 172 *(both)*

Courtesy of the Boston University Library and Mrs. Eric Hatch: 173

Photograph by the author: 183 *(both)*

Courtesy of Gloria Romanoff: 204 *(both)*

Photograph by Betty Furness: 206 *(both)*, 209 *(both)*, 210, 211, 215

Courtesy of Mr. and Mrs. Charles Lederer: 212, 214

Photograph © 1973 by Jerome Zerbe. Reproduced from *Happy Times* by Brendan Gill and Jerome Zerbe by permission of Harcourt Brace Jovanovich, Inc.: 213

Courtesy of Frank Sinatra: 226

Leonard McCombe/Time-Life Picture Agency, © Time Inc.: 229, 230

Drawing by Wm. Hamilton, © 1973 The New Yorker Magazine, Inc.: 233